CW00822828

The Mystery

of

Land of Punt

Unravelled

Second Edition

Ahmed Ibrahim Awale

ISBN: 978-87-995208-4-8

Liibaan Publishers, Denmark, Copenhagen

Cover photo: A Puntite bust excavated from a site in Hargeisa.

Figure 1: The author donning a traditional dress

Two calico sheeting, a turban, a prayer skin thrown over the shoulder, a leather shield, a spear, a native belt and a sword strapped around the wait, a wooden water bottle, a linen cotton pouch containing the Holy Book and hung from the shoulder, a wooden Qur'an *Rihli (Somali: Rixli)* or holder, a leader band with small pouch containing some written verses of the Qur'an and worn either round the neck or the upper arm, and shoes that fit or be worn on either foot. Visible in the background are the pyramid-shaped *Naasa Hablood* twin mountains. Some of the Puntite artefacts inserted in this book were excavated in this area. *Naasa Hablood,* lies in the north-eastern suburb of Hargeisa. (Photo: Warsame Ahmed)

Ahmed Ibrahim Awale

**Figure 2: A late nineteenth century Puntite girl from Somaliland
(source: anonymous)**

"In the absence of the physical Punt, perhaps we should content ourselves with the metaphysical.

But no actual Punt site has turned up so far. This may be a case of absence of evidence rather than evidence of absence, for the archaeology of both Red Sea coasts as well as the north coast of Somalia remains in its infancy. Who knows? One day soon, some archaeological site, newly revealed tomb text, or other remains may well do what Hatshepsut's humblest sailor could have done in a few words — tell us where Punt is".

_____ Peter Tyson (2009)

Emmet Scott, *the author of Hatshepsut, Queen of Sheba,* very much influenced by Immanuel Velikovsky's hypothesis of locating Punt in Israel, and challenging the 'fairly unanimous' mainstream consensus of putting Punt at the Southern end of the Red Sea in Eritrea and Somalia, or a combination of these two places, which she even describes as 'primitive land' in Hatshepsut's time, wrote the following:

> "Yet... there is no archaeological justification for such a supposition. Not a trace of anything that could be construed as implying Egyptian rule, even substantial contact with Egypt, has ever appeared. "[1]

This book will not only counter challenge statements such as this, but also, establish a basic fact that the only location where Puntite artefacts were found so far is the northern coast of the Somali peninsula.

---

[1] Emmet Scott, Hatshepsut, Queen of Sheba. Algora Publishing (2012), p. 93

**Figure 3: A pyramid-shaped cairn, locally known 'Maguur'.
(photo: Author)**
Graves of this type are common in the mountainous and coastal areas of the Somali Peninsula. They are of great antiquity with their occupants buried in a manner which indicate the belief in afterlife whereby the graves contain funerary materials and belongings.

Table of Contents

Table of Figures

Foreword

History classes have been one of my favourite subjects in my formative years. Chronicling the history of any nation or country is a treasure for posterity to learn from the past which is a mirror to the future. Historical records are even more invaluable for those cultures that do not have much written about as is the case of Somalis.

Having lived most of my life outside the homeland, I've become more nostalgic reading about the history of the Somali peninsula. The debate surrounding the location of the Land of Punt and the relationship of the pharaohs and Somalis has always fascinated me. The more I read about the subject, the more I become hungrier. It seems that I've an innate unquenchable thirst for it.

Egyptologists all agree that the most important trading partner of the ancient Egyptians was the Land of Punt known for producing gold, aromatic resins, timber, and ivory among other things. The pharaohs revered it so much that they called it *Ta Netjer* (land of the gods). This is remarkable since most civilizations are fascinated by the pharaohs. In this case, the inverse is true. Ancient Egyptians were enchanted by the mythical Land of Punt as evidenced by their numerous and repeated expeditions.

The exact location of the Land of Punt is hotly debated and still remains a mystery. Most scholars are in agreement that Punt was located to the south-east of Egypt, most likely along the Gulf of Aden coast in the Horn of Africa in present-day Somaliland, Puntland   (Northern Somalia), Djibouti, Eritrea or Sudan. Other historians argue that it was, instead, in southern Arabia - just on the other side of the Red Sea. Some even merge the two hypotheses by contending that the territory covered both areas of the Horn of Africa and Southern Arabia on either side of the Red Sea. Each school of thought presents historical and archaeological evidence to support its thesis.

Inexplicably only a few Somali scholars have delved into the discourse on the location of the Land of Punt. It is puzzling that Somali historians have not contributed much towards the debate on the subject even though it literally has happened in their own backyard. Even in the rich oral poetry Somalis are famous for, there is – to the best of my knowledge - literally no mention of the Land of Punt. However, let me caution the reader that such omission doesn't mean anything by itself. I'll be a bit philosophical on this to drive my point through. Let us assume that a tree falls in a remote jungle where there is no living creature around. Can one claim that the tree did not make a sound since it was not heard by any living creature – animal or human?

This book written by a Somali is an attempt to fill that void on the subject matter. In my opinion, there is no better Somali than the author that I know of to get a crack at expose the location of Punt is in Somaliland. I say this because I know how passionate he is about the history and environment of the Somali peninsula. I also know that the author is a prolific writer on the peninsula's indigenous plants and environment. He's an environmentalist par excellence (sans the belligerency of some) on a personal crusade not only to preserve the peninsula's flora and fauna but also its rich history.

Not only have I been privileged to be one of the first to read the manuscript, but I've also been asked to write the foreword for the book. I must admit that I've been captivated by the wealth of information – some of it never published before - presented in the book. The author's discourse is expertly weaved with logical critique and is strongly supported by evidentiary statuettes and other circumstantial facts.

In my opinion, the arguments and the supporting facts presented in the book weigh the scale that the

Land of Punt is in the Horn of Africa, and, more specifically in Somaliland/Puntland. However, even though the arguments and facts presented in the book are credible and persuasive, it's unlikely it will put the matter to rest. At least, it is my expectation that it will generate a renaissance to motivate the current author and other academicians to research the subject matter more in depth. Any discourse on the location of the Land of Punt is a healthy contribution. Such debates – in my opinion – enrich the deliberations and bring us closer to a consensus on cracking the nut of the location of Punt.

The book has taken me back in a time machine to *Naasa Hablood* … in the backdrop of the neighbourhood where I grew up. As children, we were discouraged to play around or visit the mysterious twin mountains due to the belief that they were inhabited by Jinn. Many at times later on in life, I wondered how these majestic mountains came into being: whether they were created by God or made by man. At times, since they resembled a lot the pyramids, I would lean towards the belief that they were manmade. But it was only my personal belief. I believe in the setting of this new book in our hands the majestic Naasa Hablood is beckoning the author (and others) to conduct an archaeological study to decipher how they came into being.

Finally, I strongly urge the author to continue unearthing the rich but still hidden history that our lands hold. I'm confident that the Golis Range - bordering the Red Sea - contains archaeological treasures waiting to be discovered. The 'barefoot' archaeologists mentioned in this book discovered historical nuggets in such a short time. Just imagine how much history may be uncovered in a more sustained effort. The sky is the limit.

Mohamed Hussein H. Ali (Khan)

Punt in the Mist of Time

Since the middle of the 19th century, the exact location of the mysterious Land of Punt has been a subject of great debate among scholars – Egyptologists in particular.   Like the way raindrops erase the footmarks of a wayfarer, each of those scholars who attempted to pinpoint the probable location of the elusive Punt came up with a new hypothesis disproving his/her predecessor. As one scholar, Dmitri Meeks, who ventured into this complex issue of Punt, has phrased it, "Punt 'exists' as if in a void ... the exact whereabouts of which remain more or less unknown."[2] Also, in the words of another scholar, Jacke Phillips, "No archaeological remains have ever been identified even tentatively as Puntite." (Tyson, 2009).

In the 1850's Heinrich Karl Brugsch, having based his hypothesis on hieroglyphic texts revealed during that period, suggested that the location of the Land of Punt was situated in the Arabian Peninsula. However, after the discovery of the Deir-el-Bahri *bas-reliefs*, the opinion swung in favour of an African location. It was Auguste Mariette (1881), a French Egyptologist who challenged Brugsch's suggestion, chiefly because some of the animals depicted on

---

[2] Peter Tyson, Where is Punt, Nova 2009

Hatshepsut's *bas relief* panels at Deir-el-Bahri, such as rhinoceros and giraffes, were found in Africa. His conclusion was that Punt could not be any location other than the Somali coast which also, was known for its aromatics, including the fabled frankincense and myrrh. [3] Mariette's hypothesis has remained unchallenged for the next 80 years.

Coming to the middle of 20th century, Rolf Herzog (1968), focusing on the flora displayed on the Deir-el-Bahri reliefs, suggested that the location of Punt could be the confluence of the Blue and the White Nile in the present day Sudan. [4] Then it was Kenneth Kitchen (1971), who refuted Herzog's argument after examining the fishes and marine creatures on the reliefs, pointing them as Red Sea species and, therefore, concluded that Punt was the present day Eritrea.[5] Dmitri Meeks (2003) kicked the ball back to Arabia - particularly the areas from Yemen to the Gulf of Aqaba. [6]   Then Stanley Balanda (2005-2006) reconciled the two views proposed by Kitchen and Meeks by suggesting that Punt was on both sides of the Red Sea - specifically in the Baab-al-Mandab area.

---

[3] Mariette, *Dayr-el-Bahari*, p. 30, Hichrichs (1877).
[4] Crowther, Bete, Locating the Land of Punt – the Case for Eritrea – PhD dissertation. P. 6
[5] Ibid, p. 7
[6] Charlotte Morgan, *Where is the Land Punt*, Swansea University (2014)

Moreover, there has been even a suggestion favouring Uganda (Wicker 1998)[7], and as far as Sumatera in Indonesia[8] as the Land of Punt. In 2009, Immanuel Velikovsky, a scholar of Russian-Jewish origin, argued that Punt must have been Israel, while at the same time identified Hatshepsut with the Queen of Sheba.[9] Emmet Scott, the author of *Hatshepsut, Queen of Sheba,* also supports Velikovsky's claim. Others suggest that one should not look around the corner for Punt, guessing it might be half-way around the globe, and specifically meaning Peru in South America.[10] A more recent argument raised by three scientists in the USA zeroes it down on Eritrea after carrying out analysis on hairs taken from a mummy of a baboon (*Papio hamadryas*) which they alleged to have originated from Eritrea.[11]

In an unpublished PhD dissertation titled "Locating the Land of Punt – the Case for Eritrea", Crowther

---

[7] Wicker, F.D.P. (1998) 'The Road to Punt', Geographical Journal, vol. 164, 1976. Pp. 45-56.

[8] Dani Irwanto, Land of Punt is Sumatera. (2015)

[9] Immanuel Velikovsky, *From the Exodus to King Akhnaton: Blessed Land of Punt* (2009), p.121

[10] Rick Sanders, *Where is Punt, 'the Land of God'?* 21st Science and Technology, (Spring 2009), pp. 54-57

[11] A story on the findings of the report was widely disseminating in the internet. Also refer to an article titled: "Scientists zero in on ancient Land of Punt", by David Perlman, science editor at San Francisco Chronicle.

(2010) tirelessly attempted to convince readers that Punt could not be other than Eritrea. Yet, in his concluding remarks, he contradicts that very claim by suggesting:

> "The archaeological case for Punt being based on Eritrea is not so strong, probably because so little archaeology has been carried out so far in that troubled country, but it is as strong as the archaeological evidence for any other contender, and what there is, is supportive"[12]

Similarly, the northern Somali coast has been in a state of turmoil during the past two decades. Even before that, no major archaeological exploration has ever been carried out. Yet, the Puntite artefacts to be presented in this book usher the beginning of new history that could irrefutably put the location of the Land of Punt on the world map.

Despite the above contradicting speculations thrown by different scholars, no archaeological findings and remains (other than those to be presented in this book) has ever been identified as a Puntite or a past inhabitant of the Land of Punt. The closest indication of a possible relationship of any archaeological material with Punt is the unearthing of the remains of

---

[12] Corwther, Pete (2010), Locating the Land of Punt – the Case for Eritrea – Thesis, Certificate in Egyptology, University of Manchester. Unpublished. P. 13

ship timber, stone anchors, ropes, and other artefacts dating to the Middle Kingdom found in the ancient Egyptian Red Sea port of *Saww* (Mersa Gawasis).[13] Yet this discovery *only* alludes to that *Saww* was the port that handled the Egyptian expeditions to and fro the Land of Punt.

In the following pages, I will attempt to present unique artefacts unearthed from a location that could have never been suspected to have any historical significance. With this, I believe, Punt comes out from the mist of time and locating it becomes more credible. From this also emerges a more solid hypothesis on who were the Ancient Egyptians and their relation with the Puntites, since ancient Egyptians believed that they originated from the Land of Punt. On the other hand, this will definitely support the African scholarship on Egypt's Africanity.

It is also a rebuttal to some aspects of the Eurocentric historiography and its colonial literature which came as a product of the scientific racism of the 18th and 19th century. Such a perspective attempted to attribute the ancient Egyptians and their civilization to a

---

[13] Rodolfo Fattovich, *Egypt's trade with Punt: New discoveries on the Red Sea coast*, British Museum Studies in Ancient Egypt and Sudan 18 (2012): 1–59

Caucasoid origin. [14]   Evidence from the Judeo-
Christian literature attributed Egyptians to have
originated from Misraim (son of Ham). The
descendants of Ham were traditionally regarded, and
on the basis of the biblical literature, to be the darkest
skinned branch of humanity, mainly due to
the "Curse of Ham".   However, reshaping of such
history began to take place during the beginning of
the 19th century, following the French campaign in
Egypt, led by Napoleon Bonaparte, and the
subsequent knowledge about the existence of a
civilization older than that of Rome and Greece.
Napoleon's expedition to Egypt in 1798 became the
historical catalyst that provided the Western World
with the impetus to turn the Hamite into Caucasian.[15]
However, by the 20th Century, the above hypothesis
was abandoned, but only to be replaced by new
theories mainly, the Dynastic Race Theory which,
according to Flinders Petrie proposed that
technologically superior group of elite foreigners
from Mesopotamia invaded Egypt and caused the rise
of the Dynastic Civilization. [16]   There was also a

---

[14] Edith Sanders: *The Hamitic hypothesis: its origin and functions in time perspective*, The Journal of African History, Vol. 10, No. 4 (1969), pp. 521–532
[15] Ibid. p 532
[16] Flinders Petrie (1853-1942) who came up with this 'Dynastic Race' theory after carrying out archaeological excavations in massive ancient burial site near the village

modified version of the above theories which maintained that the descendants of Ham were Caucasians (contrary with the Biblical interpretation) and, hence, are the ones who brought civilization to Egypt. A more radical hypothesis is the Caucasoid Race Theory claiming that Egypt was originally peopled by a branch of the Caucasian race,[17] and acknowledged that Negroes were present in ancient Egypt but claimed they were either captives or servants.'[18]

Along a similar vein, David Rohl, in his *Legend – the Genesis of Civilization*, maintains Flinders Petrie's hypothesis of 'superior' elites from Mesopotamia as the founders of Ancient Egyptian civilization and confirming the route of the migration through the Horn of Africa and finally the Red Sea en route to Egypt.

> This Falcon tribe had certainly originated in Elam (Susiana), as indicated by the hero and lions on the Araq knife handle.[19] They went down the Persian

---

of Nakada about 20 miles north of Luxor in Upper Egypt in 1894-95.

[17] Bruce Baum, The Rise and Fall of the Caucasian Race: A Political History of Racial Identity, p. 108

[18] Morton, Samuel George (1844). "Egyptian Ethnography".

[19] Araq knife handle (Gebel el-Arak knife), an ivory and flint knife dating from the Naqada II d period of Egyptian

Gulf and settled in 'the Horn of Africa." There they name the "Land of Punt," sacred to later Egyptians as the source of the race. The Pun people founded the island fortress of Ha-fun which commands the whole of the coast, and hence came the Punic or Phenic peoples of classical antiquity ... Those who went up the Red Sea formed the dynastic invaders of Egypt entering by the Kuseir-Koptos road. Others went to Syria and founded Tyre, Sidon and Aradus, named after their home islands in the Persian Gulf.

In the above, Flinders Petrie confirms that the Somali coast was the Land of Punt, as 'it was the Punic or Phenic peoples who founded the island fortress of Ha-fun' (*Haafuun* in Somali), but fails to make any mention of neither African presence nor contribution in the Horn of Africa that could have an imprint on the Ancient Egyptian civilization.

---

prehistory, starting circa 3450 BC, believed to be showing Mesopotamian influence.

A brief background of archaeological works in the Somali Peninsula

Archaeological excavations in the Somali peninsula are still in its infancy. However, it is worth noting that some important reconnaissance works have been carried out in the past by a number of people, most notably, A.T. Curle (1937) in his *'The Ruined Towns of Somaliland'* and N. Chittick (1974) in his *'An Archaeological Reconnaissance of the Horn: The British-Somali Expedition'*. Through the Somali government support, Chittick led an archaeological expedition in the north-eastern part of Somalia, with emphasis on Cape Guardafui at the eastern tip of the Horn. The reconnaissance mission found numerous examples of historical artefacts and structures, including ancient coins, Roman pottery, cairns etc. Many of the finds were of pre-Islamic era and associated with the ancient settlements described in the 1st Century A.D. Peripuls of the Erythraean Sea.[20]

Those archaeological studies in the Somali peninsula revealed ruined cities, pyramid-like cairns (*Maguuro*), stonewalls, and unglazed shards of pottery, along with the ruined wall construction of *Warqaade*, all pointing to a sophisticated culture that at one time thrived on the region. The studies have also revealed

[20] http://en.wikipedia.org/wiki/Neville_Chittick

that the Puntites developed a system of writing that is
yet to be decoded by scientists. Moreover, the result
of the various studies carried out in the region has
revealed that Punt was engaged in commercial
relations with the ancient Egyptians, Mycenaeans,
and Greeks since the second millennium BCE.[21]

Earlier, in 1896, Seton-Karr found at a location
situated approximately 90 km west of the port town
of Berbera, at a location called '*Issutugan*', Acheulio-
sevallvisian artefacts, which is said to be the most
ancient collection of its kind from the Horn of Africa.
Sir John Evans, writing on the subject matter in his
'*On some Palaeolithic implements found in Somaliland by
H. W. Seton-Karr*" opined that these discoveries
seemed to him to have so wide an interest, and such
an important bearing on the question of the original
home of the human race. He concluded his paper
with this interesting remark:

> "That the cradle of the human family must have
> been situated in some part of the world where the
> climate was genial, and the means of subsistence
> readily obtained, seems almost self-evident; and that
> these discoveries in Somaliland may serve to
> elucidate the course by which human civilization,
> such as it was, If not indeed the human race,

---

[21] Raphael Chijioke Njoku, *The History of Somalia*, (2013)
Greenwood Books.

proceeded westward from its early home in the east is a fair subject for speculation."[22]

In the recent years, the archaeology of the region received some international interest, following the uncovering of Laas Geel and Dhambalin rock art – the former by Prof. Xavier Gutherz and his team from Montpellier III University in 2002[23], and the later by Sada Mire, a Somali archaeologist, for her discovery of Dhambalin rock art in 2008.[24]

Now, I like would raise the following questions: Why it is so important to locate the Land of Punt? And why so much search effort has been put into it and still taking place? The above two question can also be directly linked with another question: What race were the ancient Egyptians? A straight-forward answer is that the Land of Punt is where ancient Egyptians originated. E.A. Wallis Budge confirming this claims said "Egyptian tradition of the Dynastic Period held that the aboriginal home of the Egyptians was

---

[22] Sir John Evans, On Palaeolithic Implements found in Somaliland, H. W. Seton-Karr.

[23] Gutherz et. al. *The discovery of new rock paintings in the Horn of Africa : the rock shelters of Laas Geel, Republic of Somaliland* / Xavier Gutherz, Jean-Paul Cros & Joséphine Lesur. - 2003. -

[24] Sada Mire, The Discovery of Dhambalin Rock Art Site, Somaliland 2008).

Punt...";[25] and historians point out that the Egyptians always seemed to be able to remember the way to Punt, even when there had been long periods without contact between the two peoples.

Therefore, on the basis of the popular theory that ancient Punt was the point of origin of the builders of one of the greatest civilizations on earth, the abode of gods (according to ancient Egyptians) and a place they were enchanted with, justifies such a great interest for its search.

The case for the Somali Region

Despite the importance of the northern Somali coast in the search of the mysterious Land of Punt, the region has not had merited attention for a thorough archaeological investigation. However, the discovery of Neolithic cave paintings in a number of sites in Somaliland in 2002 - most notably Laas Geel – has created a new interest among many scholars of ancient history to direct their attention to the region. In 2002, a team consisting of French archaeologists

---

[25] E.A. Wallis Budge, *Short History of the Egyptian People* 1914, Kessinger Publishing.

from Montpellier University brought the wonders of Laas Geel to the limelight.[26]

Taking into account the recent developments in the archaeology of this region which is still in its infancy and some popular Somali myths which predate Islam as well, there seem to be a strong connection between ancient Egypt and the north-eastern part of the Horn of Africa. As a starting point, there is an striking similarity between Hathor (see below), one of the most famous ancient Egyptian goddesses, and the themes of the Neolithic rock painting found at Laas Geel, which depict, among other things, personages worshipping cows. Another comparison can be made between the popular Somali myth of a bull balancing the universe on its horns, on one hand, and a similar depiction of Hathor carrying a golden sun on its horns, on the other.

---

[26] Gutherz, Xavier et a., *Mission Report, the Rock Shelters of the Laas Geel Site (2003)*

Figure 4: Egyptian goddess Hathor carrying the sun on its horns and suckling Hatshepsut, Deir-el-Bahri, Egypt

Figure 5: One of the dozens of Neolithic cave paintings depicting cow worshippers at Laas Geel, Somaliland (Photo: Author)cow worshippers at Laas Geel, Somaliland (Photo: Author)

According to an old tradition, the Land of Punt was the abode of the gods who migrated thence, with

Amon, Horus, and Hathor, into the Nile Valley.[27] This might be the reason why the name Land of Punt is synonymous with the Land of gods (*Ta netjer*). According to Edouard Naville (d. 1926), a Swiss archaeologist and Egyptologist, this is what the inscription on one of the sculptured scene at Deir el Bahri, which recorded the presents from Egypt to Punt, reads: *"All good things"* (from Egypt) *"are brought by the order of Her Majesty's to Hathor, the Lady of Punt."*

There is also a close resemblance between the humpless cattle (*Bos taurus*) of *Laas Geel* rock panels (above) and those of Punt sculptured on the walls of Deir-el-Bahri, which can be seen resting in the shade. Currently, this humpless species is not found anywhere in either Somaliland/Somalia or Ethiopia. However, Mohamed Diriye Abdullahi, a Somali-Canadian scholar, linguist and writer, citing Brandt et. al (1983, p.16), wrote about rock shelters at Karin Heegane, a natural mountain pass approximately 70 kilometres southwest of Bosaso in north-eastern Somalia, which contain extensive rock paintings. He argued that the important feature (of the cave paintings) is a type of humpless cattle, today extinct

---

[27] The Land of Punt. An article which appeared in the New York Times, April 27, 1879

in the Somali peninsula, but found in Egypt, called *Jamuusa*.[28]

I will elucidate later how the gradual process of drying and progressive aridity in the Horn of Africa turned the once lush and Eden-like environment into the present day condition. The iconographic representation of the camel in *God-hardhane* (*God Xardhane*) in Somaliland may shed some light on the increase in aridity. Its domestication and introduction[29] into the region was a response to the effects progressive aridity.

'Frankincense Terraces' of Punt

The physical features of the north-eastern coast of modern day Somaliland and Puntland conform to the 'frankincense terraces of Punt' as these gum-bearing trees and shrubs are still found on terraced stands locally known as *laag*. It is worth noting here how the magnificent three terrace (one above the other) Deir el

---

[28] Mohamed Diriye Abdullahi, *"Cushites of North-eastern Africa: Stone Age Origins to Iron Age,"* in Kevin Shillington (ed.), Encyclopaedia of African History, Fitzroy Dearborn, 2004.

[29] As advocated by Bulliet (1975), camels were present in Africa during pre-Roman times. They first entered Africa through southern Arabia and the Horn of Africa. K.O. Farah et.al, *The Somali and the Camel: Ecology, Management and Economics.* Anthropologist, 6(1): 45-55 (2004)

Bahri building was designed to mimic the physical feature of the 'terraces of Punt' seen in the next picture. Also among the most valuable treasures brought from Punt were the thirty-two incense-bearing trees for 'the god's garden'. Queen Hatshepsut, in fulfilment of the instructions of god Amon to make at his house a garden so large that he could walk therein, and, therefore, at his command she equipped an expedition to fetch incense-bearing trees from the land of Punt, the country of the Gods, in obedience to the word of Amon to make 'a Punt in my house (temple) or a second Punt in his garden'.[30] The aim of the expedition was to transport myrrh and frankincense trees, and then replant in Egypt for religious purposes, so as to reduce the cost of procuring the items. However, the mission failed, as the climate of Egypt did not facilitate the ideal conditions for their survival and productivity.

According to N. F. Hepper of the Royal Botanical Gardens (Kew), quoted by Sayed Abdel Monem, a prominent Egyptian Egyptologist, the species of frankincense prevailing in these places are *Boswellia carteri* and *Boswellia frereana* which have been found in

---

[30] Marie Luise Schroeter Gothein, *A History of Garden Art: From the Earliest Times to the Present Day* (Cambridge Library Collection - Botany and Horticulture) (Volume 1) Paperback – September 11, 2014. P. 17

Egyptian tombs.[31] *Boswellia frereana* is only found in those north-eastern mountain ranges facing the Gulf of Aden. Today, the frankincense and myrrh yielding areas of the Somali peninsula are still extensive and gum collection and sale is a common practice.

Other than the Myrrh (*commiphora myrhha*), out of the many species of Frankincense, found in Africa and parts of Arabia, viz. *Boswellia carteri, Boswellia frereana, Boswellia rivae, Boswellia papyrifera,* and *Boswellia bhau-dajiana*, the first two, are found in the north-eastern mountainous part of the Somali region, not far from the coast of the Gulf of Aden, and produce the most and highest quality resins. *Bowellia rivae* is also found in the Somali Region of Ethiopia. The proximity of where *Boswellia carterii* and *Boswellia frereana* grow to the coast and the comparatively higher quantity and quality of their resin deemed necessary for burning as an offering to the gods, makes the Somali coast the most likely place of the Land of Punt.

The African Pencil Cedar (*Juniperus procera*) is also found on the evergreen forest formation ecological zone starting from 1,500m above sea level. (Hemming, 1966). There is a consensus among Egyptologists that the timber used by ancient Egyptians for shipbuilding was made from cedar trees growing on the mountains of the eastern

---

[31] Sayed, A. M. A. H., (2003). The Land of Punt: Problems of the Archaeology of the Red Sea and the South-eastern Delta, University of Alexandria.

Mediterranean and the main port that handled the exportation of the cedar was Byblos of the Phoenicians.[32] Another riparian tree which is used for boat building, found along the banks of the seasonal watercourse on the coastal Somali plains is *Conocarpus lancifolius*, locally known as *'dhamas'*.[33] Its wood is light in colour and density and has a long life in salt water. Formerly its chief importance was in building Arab sailing ships (dhows) and timber cut in Somalia was worked in Arabia.[34] The timber from the tree is also ideal for making ship masts.

---

[32] Cheryl Ward, *Building pharaoh's ships: Cedar, incense and sailing the Great Green*. British Museum Studies in Ancient Egypt and Sudan 18 (2012): 217–32
[33] Biodiversity Research in the Horn of Africa, Proceedings of the Third International symposium on the Flora of Ethiopia and Eritrea, Carlsberg Academy (2001), pg. 144
[34] Report on an environmental experiment, by Rene D. Haller (Mombasa, 1974)

Figure 6: Terraced Daalo Mountains immediately south of Maydh
coastal town (known during the time of the Periplus as Mundus).
(Photo: Author)

Those mountain terraces (*Laagag*) are orientated in an
east-west direction and can be found all along the
Golis Range which runs parallel with the Gulf of
Aden. In some areas, the maritime plain between the
mountain range and the sea becomes narrower as one
moves to the east whereby in some locations the
mountains touch the sea.[35] Sayed, visited the north-
eastern Somali coast, and draws the physical
similarity between that area and the ancient Punt. He
also described Punt as a coastal hilly country where
the frankincense trees grow on terraces very near to
the seashore. (Sayed 2003). Within the same

---

[35] C.F. Hemming, The Vegetation of Somaliland, 1966,
Proceedings of the Linnaean Society of London

ecological zone, we find the *Xiis* tree (*Pistacia aethiopica Kokwaro*) which exudes *Murkud* gum[36], most probably the *Mocrotu* incense that has been in use for over 2,000 years as recorded in the pages of *the Periplus of the Erythraean Sea*. Syed concludes his argument with this:

> "… We can conclude that the physical feature of North Eastern Somaliland and its production of frankincense did not change for 2,000 years (between the time of the *Periplus* and the present day). Consequently, it was nearly the same for the 1,500 years before the time of the Periplus (i.e. in the time of Queen Hatshepsut)." (Sayed 2003)

In the same area, on the coast, lies the town of Mait (*Maydh*), mentioned in *the Periplus* as *Mundus* where the above mentioned *Mocrotu* incense was exported. *Mait* must have been the *Matoi* found in the Egyptian records. The word is mentioned in the following

---

[36] The '*Murkud*' (Mocrotu?) gum is burned as incense. Believed to be an evil warder, the soft exudate is pressed in the folds of the ears of a new born bay. In Oman, the root of the *Pistacia lentiscus* is dried and crushed into powder, mixed with water, and then a piece of iron inserted. According to local tradition, the preparation is used as an evil warder, evil eye, and exorcism. The liquid is also taken orally by women who experienced multiple miscarriages, while a part of the root is sewed with leather and worn for the same purpose. (*Plants of Dhofar*, Anthony G. Miller p. 26).

passage which describes the importance of the main Egyptian deity "Amon":

> "The Chief of the Two Lands, great of strength, lord of might, chiefest, who made the entire earth (Lord of Karnak).   More eminent of nature than any god, over whose beauty the gods rejoice. He to whom praise is given in the Great House, who is crowned in the House of Fire. He whose sweet savour the gods love, when he cometh from Punt. Richly perfumed, when he cometh from the land of the **Matoi.** Fair of face, when he cometh from god's land".[37]

Some scholars put Matoi[38] in an area in the eastern desert of Nubia.[39]   But the last sentence qualifies that Matoi was god's land, which in turn means the Land of Punt. Hence, Mait (*Maydh*) is more likely be the Matoi, which is situated in the *Waaqooyi* (the Land of gods). Therefore, the land of Matoi can be strongly

---

[37] Ancient Egyptians Literature: A sourcebook of their Writings. Edited by Adolf Erman (1966), p. 284

[38] The northern part of the Somali peninsula is called 'Waqooyi/Waaqooyi). The word also a direction and is, therefore, corresponds with 'north'.   The word is a derivative of Waaq (the Cushitic sky-god).   Therefore, we can confidently say that 'waaqooyi' is synonymous with 'Ta Netjer' or the Land of Gods.

[39] Albright, William Foxwell (1940), From the Stone Age to Christianity: Monotheism and the Historical Process. John Hopkins Press.

inferred to that the Somali coast which is the Land of Punt.

Mohamed Hussein Abby, a Somali scholar, in his paper, *The Land of Poun* (Punt)[40], while commenting on the above passage writes the following:

"I can't fail to notice the connection alluded to in the above passage between "the savour of Punt", "the rich perfume of the land of the Matoi" and "the fair face of god's land" from which the god Amon comes. The "savour" and the "rich perfume" of these places denote the odours of Poun, which the early Egyptians called the land of the gods, because of her incense and other aromatic gums and woods. But where does the word "Matoi" come from? The word "Matoi" closely resembles the word "Maydi or Maydh", which is the place that produced the incense and other aromatic gums. The word "Matoi" cannot be other than a corruption of the word "Maydh". The bringing together of the three places (Punt, Motoi and god's land), which shows their close relationship, therefore, proves beyond any doubt that Maydh, a port in eastern Somaliland, was not only part of the ancient sacred land of Poun from which the early Egyptians came, both gods (religion)

_____

[40] Mohamed Hussein Abby (2009), *The Land of Poun (Punt)*

and men, but also had a special place and importance in the incense trade."

Ancient Egyptians believed that the gods endowed the Land of Punt with special resources such as, myrrh, frankincense, medicinal plants - products ancient Egyptians used for religious rituals, sanitation, health, and embalming dead bodies, particularly those of dead pharaohs. They also imported gold, spices, animals (like elephants and monkeys) obtained from the coast or hinterland of Punt. One of the earliest Egyptian expeditions to Punt took place around 2250 BC during the reign of pharaoh Sahure (2708-2697 BC) of the Fifth Dynasty. An inscription of his reign records that his fleet returned with 8,000 undefined measures of myrrh, 6,000 measures of 'electrum' and 2600 staves of some costly local wood.[41] Trade between Punt and Egypt continued from that era to 600 B.C., only interrupted for 200 years (roughly between 1800 B.C. and 1552 B.C.), when the Hyksos (considered by Egyptians as destructive foreign invaders) sacked the eastern Nile Delta and rose to power.

---

[41] Richard Pankhurt, the Ethiopian Borderlands: Essays in Regional History from Ancient Times to the End of the 18th Century, p. 5. The Red Sea Press Inc. (1997) Asmara, Eritrea

The Punt Homes

The people of Punt lived in round beehive shaped houses raised on stilts. Ladders were also depicted learning against the structures. This could mean that the Puntites lived in space higher than the ground level as a protection from marauding carnivores, poisonous reptiles and floods. Interestingly, the sandy coastal areas of the Somali coast are known for its abundance of snake species which kill annually dozens of pastoralists and coastal dwellers.

The Punt homes greatly resemble the traditional collapsible and portable Somali *Aqal* woven from poles, bent sticks, and covered with hides and fibre mats.

Figure 7: Depiction of a Punt home as seen on the walls of Deir el Bahri.

In the above Deir-el-Bahri panel, other than the Punt homes, branching palm trees can be seen. There are many species of palm trees found in the northern coastal areas of the Somali Peninsula. Doum palm *(Hyphaene thebaica)* is found on coastal areas, while 'Maydho' *(Phoenix reclinata)* and date palm *(Phoenix dactylifera)* are found along the seasonal water course in the *Guban* (coastal and sub-coastal) areas. Another palm species found inland on higher mountainous grounds in Somaliland/Puntland and Djibouti as well is Livistona palm *(Livistona carienensis)*, known in Somali as *Madaah/Daabaan*.[42]

Hargeisa and its Hidden Treasures

In the following pages I will attempt to narrate what could be the most sensational piece of history since the discovery of the Rosetta stone in late 18th century which helped decipher Egyptian Hieroglyphics. [43] Priceless artefacts from the past were first unearthed from a most unlikely place in February 2012. This is no other place than Hargeisa, the capital of Somaliland and its surrounding areas. I inserted here below the pictures of some of the objects dug from a number of sites on a mountain slope known as *Gol*

---

[42] In Djibouti, the tree is known as Bankouale palm.
[43] It was Jean Francois Champollion, who in 1822 first deciphered the Rosetta Stone and Egyptian hieroglyphics.

Waraabe located just not more than 1 km from Hargeisa Airport and other location in the Golis Range mountain areas, including *Naasa Hablood* – the twin pyramid-shaped mountains. The latter are the unmistakable landmarks of Hargeisa. Truly, no one could have entertained the idea that such objects of antiquity and historical significance could be found there.

Hargeisa is situated approximately 120 km inland to the south of the nearest coastal point at Bulahar town, and 158 km from the well-known port town of Berbera – the Malao of *the Periplus of the Erythraean Sea*. Hargeisa lies on a V-shaped valley, circa 1334m above sea level, and bisected by *Maroodi Jeex* seasonal watercourse which empties its water into the Gulf of Aden. A range of hills which reach a maximum altitude of 200-250 m above the valley bottom run parallel with the seasonal water course in an east-west direction. Until the recent discovery of what I will call here "Puntite" artefacts, no trace of civilization was reported in that area in the hinterland of Somaliland. Hargeisa was founded only during the 1880's as recorded in the annals of the European travellers who used to traverse the once forested ground and savannah plains teaming with wildlife of great diversity. Lord Delamere made his first trip to Somaliland in 1891 to hunt lions, and returned on a yearly basis to resume the hunt, before his final departure to Kenya in 1896 with a retinue consisting of dozens of stalwart Somalis and 200 camels. [44] Standing at a vantage point on the southern high ground of the valley and facing towards the north-eastern direction, one can see the captivating twin mountains of *Naasa hablood,* 'Maidens Breasts' – named so because of their likeliness to the bosom of a maiden.

In the distant past, the Somali Peninsula was covered with thick forests, permanent rivers and teeming with a wide variety of wild life. The prolificacy of its flora and fauna has been reported even as recent as the middle of the nineteenth century. [45]   As will be indicated in the following paragraph, the presence of a limestone bust carved into the shape of a crocodile among the many artefacts found in Hargeisa, could possibly mean that *Maroodi Jeex* seasonal water course was a permanent river, sometime in the distant past. Moreover, as those artefacts were unearthed from the upper reaches of the valley top that may also indicate that impenetrable forests covered the whole valley bottom, while the higher grounds afforded space for

---

[44] Bull, Bartle. (1992). *Safari: A Chronicle of Adventure,* p. 188.
[45] Descriptions of the richness of flora and fauna of Somaliland during the late 19th century is well documented in the works of many European travellers such as Major Swayne's *Seventeen Trips through Somaliland* (pg291),

habitation for the Puntites. Positioning their dwellings on those vantage points had many advantages namely, reconnaissance against enemies – be it human or wild animal, and possibly for its health benefits compared to the marshy and forested areas down in the valley, so as to reduce the risk of contracting waterborne diseases - such as malaria, etc. Interestingly, Somalis have known before the Europeans that mosquitoes cause malaria. Richard Burton, the explorer, in a work published in 1856, told of a tribe in Somaliland among whom the superstition was current that mosquito bites caused fatal fevers, and the native superstition proved forty years later to be correct.[46] Thereafter, the predominant belief in Europe and North America that such 'fatal fevers' was caused by bad air, and hence 'Mal aria', was proven wrong.

The mysterious land of Punt was a source of gold. Yet again, the presence of this precious metal in locations not far from Hargeisa is another indicator that could relate the Somali Peninsula to Punt. Arabsio is only 30 km west of Hargeisa and has been identified during the middle of last century by British

---

[46] E. Ashworth Underwood, Malaria in History. An article in the Spectator Archive, 19 July, 1946; also reported in Major Swayne's *Seventeen Trips Through Somaliland*, pg. 154.

geological surveyors as a potential site for gold prospecting. In 2011, the Nubian Gold Cooperation - a Canadian based exploration company - signed an agreement with the relevant Ministry in Somaliland to prospect for gold in the area.

Queen Hatshepsut's expedition to the Land of Punt brought back a lot of gold. Unfortunately, her record does not mention the mining regions of Punt, apart from Amu. The knowledge we so far have on the origins of gold from Punt is scanty or not established yet, but according to Eric Robson - the author of *In Search of Queen Hatshepsut's Land of Marvels* - who laments the inaccuracies that could result from transliteration and spelling of foreign place names - he believes that *Amu* might be synonymous with *Nemyew* - a gold producing region probably in the western borderlands of Ethiopia[47]. In my analysis, *Amu* could be *Amud* valley near Borama town, which is located only 90 km west of Hargeisa. *Amud* lies in Awdal region of Somaliland where gemstone prospecting has been going on during the past two decades or so.[48] In 2014, a Chinese company started work in earnest to extract gemstone varieties such as,

---

[47] Eric Robson, Queen Hatshepsut's Land of Marvels, p.34
[48] Also read the article: Rich gemstone potentials found in Somaliland.
http://weerar.wordpress.com/2008/03/16/rich-gemstone-potentials-discovered-in-somaliland/

sapphire, emeralds, heliodor (green beryl), aquamarine, etc in that area.[49]   It is more likely that *Amud (Amu)* served as a transit centre for the products coming from the more productive hinterland (which later became to be known as Ethiopia) on the way to Gulf of Aden for shipment to Egypt. The distance of Amud from Ethiopian-Somali border is only 5 km.   Amud also remained an important trading centre during the middle ages linking Zeila (Avalities of the Periplus) to the Ethiopian hinterland. The synonymy of *Amud* with *Amu*, as a transit centre for gold, is further qualified by Richard Pankhurt's statement, in which he argues that the gold destined for Egypt originated from Ethiopia:

> "Egyptian inscriptions and pictorial reliefs dating from the early times indicate the objects which the Land of Punt supplied to the Pharaohs. Such goods included gold, doubtless from the Ethiopian interior, ivory and panther and other skins, which could have come almost from anywhere in the region, and myrrh and myrrh trees, and ostrich feathers, probably originating from the African coastal belt."[50]

---

[49] Somalilandpress (new item: Dec. 11, 2014)
[50] Richard Pankhurst, the Ethiopian Borderlands: Essays in Regional History from Ancient Times to the End of the 18th Century, p. 3. The Red Sea Press Inc. (1997) Asmara, Eritrea

Amud (Amu) was a centre of substantial trade activities in the past, and is counted as one of many ruined ancient towns in Somaliland and lies on the route from the eastern sections of the Ethiopian highlands to the coastal town of Zeila. A university carrying the same name stands now in the valley in an area adjacent to the rubbles of the ancient town.

Sensational Discovery of Puntite Artefacts in the valley of Hargeisa

One afternoon, in late December, 2012, a group of treasure hunters took a short trip to the *Gol Waraabe* valley in Hargeisa, the capital of Somaliland. The valley top lies only 1 km to the north of the city's airport. Hargeisa has been expanding quickly in all directions since the past two decades, where even the steep grounds of the V-shaped valley are now dotted with buildings and land plot markings and foundations walls. As if guided by a remote sensing machine, a young man whom his companions address him a Sufi,[51] led the team to one of four sites with no visible physical traces or markings and not different from the surrounding areas. The site looked as if it has not been touched since creation. Then the 'Sufi' beckoned the hand tool wielding group to dig a

---

[51] In this context, the title 'Sufi' does not necessarily reflect high religious erudition or status.

specific location after solemnly pronouncing the holy formula *"Bismi-Laah!"* {In the name of Allah}. This was followed by a short supplication (*dua*) incanted by the 'sufi'. All with raised hands, they repeatedly interspersed the prayers with *"Ameen"*.

There is a strong belief among Somalis of the existence of treasures guarded and owned by Jinn that could cast harm upon or curse on any one who disturbs trespasses and/or vandalizes any ancient burial ground. Also popular among the people, is the belief that 'communion' and cooperation of the two beings (humans and jinn) can occur whereby the former will have access to hidden information on a mental and spiritual level. Sometimes, this cannot pass without harm. Many treasure seekers are believed to have been bewitched and harmed by Jinn – a phenomenon which can be compared with the Pharaoh's Curse. To minimize any risk which could result from such trespasses into the 'property' of jinn, some offerings in the form of casting a small amount of dry food or sugar in the location, or slaughtering an animal, is superstitiously believed to ward off any detriment. In concurrence with the precepts of Islamic jurisprudence, hidden treasures found, particularly precious metals and stones are sanctified through the payment of one fifth (*khums*) of what has been realized as a *Zakah*[52] to be paid to the poor and the needy.[53]

After having unearthed some artefacts from the first site, the team repeated the same technique in recovering antiquity material from the other three sites. On average, the depths of the dug holes were not more than 1m. In total, the team unearthed 24 pieces consisting of statuettes reminiscent of the ancient Egyptian artefacts, huge stone spoons very similar to the traditional Somali wooden spoon *'Fandhaal'*, *terra cotta* bowels cupped with covers made from the same material, and a peculiar looking stone made into the form of a vulture.

In my analysis, the bowels made from pottery which were cupped with the same material may have served similar purpose to the canopic jars used by the ancient Egyptians during the mummification and burial of the dead. The Egyptian equivalents were commonly either carved from limestone or were made of pottery. Interestingly, in one site near

---

[52] Payment made under Islamic law on certain kinds of property and used for charitable and religious purposes.
[53] For a detailed elucidation on the complex issue of antiquity excavation with the assistance of jinn, it is worth reading a study by Salah Hussein Al-Houdalieh, Archaeological Heritage and Spiritual Protection: Looting and the Jinn in Palestine, Journal of Mediterranean Archaeology 25.1 (2012) 99-120.

Hargeisa, the author found four *terra cotta* bowels cupped with covers made from the same material - three of them empty and the fourth containing small pieces of quartz stones (see fig. # 10) – from a shallow depth below the ground surface. The jars may have the same funerary function as practiced by ancient Egyptians in preparing the deceased for the afterlife whereby the internal parts of the body could be removed without endangering a person's chances of survival in the afterlife. The organs were treated differently according to their importance. The brain was removed and discarded, as its importance and function were apparently not understood. The heart was left in place, as it was considered the centre of intelligence and vital for survival in the next life. Other internal organs were often removed, while the lungs, liver, stomach, and intestines were singled out for special treatment, perhaps because of their links to nourishment. These organs were preserved, wrapped separately, and stored close to the coffin. A set of four Canopic Jars made from stone, pottery, or wood was often used for this purpose. Even when the internal organs were not removed or were placed back into the mummified body, a set of jars was often still placed in the burial. This is thought to indicate the importance of the jars, not just as containers, but as magical protection for the organs wherever they were.[54]

The excavation process of those artefacts was not free from challenges. The site is located within plots of privately owned land – even though uninhabited at the time of the digging. Therefore, the group was subject to the curious looks of passer byes residing in the valley bottom since the whole area is almost bare of vegetation. However, the team's success in carrying out the operation, and being not interrupted or chased out of the area, could be attributed to an intentional misleading story they concocted. A word spread in the neighbourhood that the group were carrying out landmine clearance work. Also the fact that the team leader was dressed in military uniform caused the story to pass without much scrutiny. Even so, the incident got reported to the police.

The group, along with their find, ended up in a police station near the airport. Luckily, and thanks to the efforts of some influential friends, they were released, carrying with them the pieces.

For the sake of scrutiny, the author has put the 'Sufi' to test on three different occasions on different locations and intervals - one time in the presence of

---

[54]   www.prm.ox.ac.uk/thedead.html

two other persons. In all sites, I was giving great attention to whether the ground was disturbed or soft enough to raise suspicion of deceitful act. Again, all the sites (one rocky and two gravelly) seemed as if they have not been disturbed since creation. Strangely enough, there was nothing to indicate past human activity on the ground surface; not even any of the numerous cairns (*Maguuro*) that can be conspicuously seen in many parts of the country (see fig. 3 on page 7). Before we started digging the first site, I asked the 'Sufi' what the site could contain whereby he immediately, and without hesitation, told us that it contained four sets of small burned mud bowels, each set consisting of two pieces, one cupped on the other. Again, my desire to learn what is in store for me soared high when he told us that one of the four hidden pairs of mud bowels contains something within them! The shocking revelation came true after we finished from digging the site.

From the other two sites, we retrieved two statuettes, one of which is on the cover page of this book.

Ahmed Ibrahim Awale

Figure 8: Site 1 to be dug with one of my accomplices holding the digging bar.

Figure 9: (after digging): Four sets of mud bowels, one of each cupped on the other

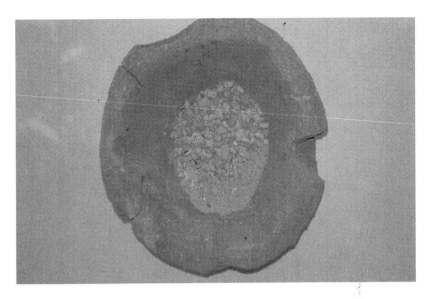

Figure 10: Some stones, mainly of quartz type in one of the four sets of mud bowels as to by the 'Sufi' before digging.

A Closer look at the Puntites and their environment

Some of artefacts found in the area may indicate the existence of an aquatic civilization that thrived in the region thousands of years ago. Therefore, it can be inferred that the land must have been thickly forested. The depiction of crocodile heads on the skulls of human statuettes indicates the presence of these creatures (see fig. 16). The elongated skull or 'cone-heads, a characteristic feature which was popular among the Pharaohs and seen as a symbol of status, high rank, or wisdom, is also repeated in some

Puntite figurines. Here, it was the crocodile, and not the lion (so called the king of the jungle) that crowded the psyche of the "Puntites". This may also indicate that the north-eastern Horn was a part of the aquatic civilization of middle Africa made possible by wetter climate during the period between tenth and third millennia B.C.[55]   The valley of Hargeisa, starting from its upper catchment area at *Aaraale* and *Arra Madow*, and skirting past *Gadka-Yogol*, down to the lower lands of *Aw Barkhadle* and beyond, might have been covered with dense forests. Even the barren, rocky and dreary looking mountain sides where some of the Puntite artefacts were found might have been covered with rich soil and lush tropical montane forest.

Climate change, decrease of precipitation and the prominence of the bi-model rainfall patterns whereby two rainy seasons (*Gu'* and *Deyr*) are alternated by two dry seasons (*Xagaa* and *Jilaal*) had a desiccating effect on the flora and fauna as well as their composition and distribution. While myriads of species have been banished by climate change, new ones established themselves within the changing ecosystems, while many others also adapted

---

[55] Sutton, J. E. G., *the Aquatic Civilization of Middle Africa*, Journal of African History, XV, 4, (1974), pp 527-524

themselves to the ever-changing environmental conditions.

On the basis of the foregoing, in an attempt to locate the exact location of the Land of Punt, many scholars – probably overlooking the impact of climate change on the succession of species and changes in their distribution, have fallen in the pitfall of judging a location simply on the presence and/or absence of certain animals and plants in a particular area. My argument is that archaeological evidence can be the best criterion (rather than plant and animal species) that can make a breakthrough and put this long-standing argument to rest. Plants and animals adapt to climatic changes, while buried, then later discovered artefacts tell the hidden mysterious history of any land. So far, although the Puntite artefacts require a thorough investigation and proper archaeological excavations, yet, I presume that they pose a strong argument to prove and to mark the Land of Punt on the Somali peninsula.

The description, looks and physical features of the people of Punt, as depicted in Deir-el-Bahri *bas reliefs*, is strikingly similar to what we can see in our Puntite artefacts. Eric Robson describing Parehou, the Puntite chief, wrote the following:

"... Tall and similar in colour and features to the Egyptians, his nose is aquiline, he wears a beard, and his hair is carefully prepared. His dress consists of a loin cloth and a belt which a dagger is fixed, and his right leg appears to be braced and adorned with a large number of rings..." (Robson 2007).

From the above quote, one can draw a conclusion that there was a great similarity between ancient Egyptians and the Puntites.   As further matter, the fact that ancient Egyptians considered the Land of Punt as their ancestral home will not deny the likelihood that the so called two different 'races' were one and the same people.   Ancient Egyptians sometimes called Punt land *Ta-Netjer*, meaning "Land of the Gods". W. M. Flinders Petrie (d. 1942), a British archaeologist, also believed that the Dynastic Race (which had an earlier theory that the earliest roots of the ancient Egyptian Dynastic civilization were imported by invaders from Mesopotamia) came from or through Punt[56]. However, this theory has lost its mainstream support by the Egyptological community.[57] E. A. Wallis Budge also stated that "Egyptian tradition of the Dynastic Period held that

---

[56] Finders Petrie, *The Making of Egypt*" (1939) states that the Land of Punt was "sacred to the Egyptians as the source of their race."

[57] http://en.wikipedia.org/wiki/Dynastic_Race_Theory

the aboriginal home of the Egyptians was Punt..."[58]. Interestingly and paradoxically enough, in an attempt to deny the people of Punt their true identity rooted in the African continent, Eric Robson mentions that "some writers have regarded Parehou and his race as alien to the region (of Africa)."[59]   Contrarily, our Puntite personages tell a different and more reliable story. Their features are so strikingly very Somali to an extent that each one reminds me of a person whom I know or met in the streets of Hargeisa and the other towns in the country. The oval face, thin lips, aquiline nose and the slender features of the Puntites are all typically Somali.

Ancient Egyptians and Puntite Similarities

This is just the beginning, but from the above discoveries, the mystery that had shrouded the location of the Land of Punt for such a long time is in the process of being unravelled. The land of Punt was

---

[58] A. Wallis Budge, *Short History of the Egyptian People.* (1911).   Budge stated that "Egyptian tradition of the Dynastic Period held that the aboriginal home of the Egyptians was Punt..."

[59] Eric Robson, *In Search of Punt: Queen Hatshepsut's Land of Marvels*, 2007. Pg 54

also known as the 'Land of gods' – the later name still surviving in the Somali language. The Somali word *'Waqooyi or Waaqooyi'* has two meanings: a) north (as a direction); and b) the Golis Mountain range which runs parallel with the Gulf of Aden. Before the advent of Islam in the north eastern Africa, Somalis, like the other Cushites, were *Waaq* worshipers – the Cushitic Sky god. The Golis Mountains (*Waaqooyi*) clearly befits the Land of Punt criterion not only as sacred but also the source of all the favourite products of ancient Egyptians namely Myrrh, Frankincense, Gold etc. In other words, *'Waaqooyi'* could mean the 'dwelling place of gods.'

Of the many convincing features to be seen in our Puntites artefacts, I want to present the below figurine (fig. 11) which carries two symbols of authority popular among ancient Egyptians. The crook (*heka*) and the flail or flabellum (*nekhakha*), are two of the most prominent items in the royal regalia of ancient Egypt. The crook is very similar to the present-day *Hangool* – the most important tool the Somali pastoralist uses in erecting a thorn enclosure (kraal) for his livestock from tree branches. Now let us compare it with the next picture (fig. 12) which stands for the golden mask of King Tutankhamun. Both figurines display the two implements. Again both of them carry on their heads the cobra snake and the vulture as a symbol of the deities *Wadjet* and *Nekhbet*, otherwise known as the *'Two Ladies'* – worshipped by all after the unification of Lower Egypt and Upper Egypt. Both goddesses were retained because of the importance of their roles and the belief that they were the protectors of unified Egypt.[60]

The royal cobra (*uraeus*) was worn by the pharaohs over their brows. It was the symbol of supreme rulers, and a symbol of Pharaoh's power. It was thought to spit fire at the pharaoh's enemies. The *uraeus* was also thought to possess magical powers since Egyptians believed it to be the magical eye of the god Horus.[61] Another similarity between the mask of Tutankhamun and the Puntite relief figurine is what is called the divine osird beard which in death, the kings were frequently portrayed wearing it.

The Somali word for bird is *'shinbir'*. The word is also interpreted as 'a new lease of life', 'recovery from a terminal disease' or a 'harbinger and a medium that brings good tidings relating to the recovery of a sick person'. For example if a person is terminally ill and nothing to support his/her recovery can be arranged for him/her, Somalis say *'hebel shinbir ma laha'*

---

[60] Toby A. H. Wilkinson, *Early Dynastic Egypt*, Routledge 1999, p. 292

[61] Currid, 148; Hans Biedermann, *Dictionary of Symbolism* (NY, NY: Meridian, 1994), 311.

(literally, that man has/she no bird' which means he 'has no luck to continue living', but in case he/she miraculously recovers from illness with a potion concocted by someone, and thereafter, the later recovers, people say *'Waxaas baa hebel Shinbir looga soo dhigay'*, {the action of such person or thing was a *shinbir* for the sick person to recover}. It is worth noting here that the Somali term *'shinbir'* is meant for both male and female bird, but with slight difference in pronunciation. Likewise, the Egyptian *ba* is a winged spirit of a blessed dead person. Depicted with the body of a bird and head of the deceased, the *ba* was able to fly from the underworld to visit, unseen, the world of the living.[62]

Yet, another striking similarity between the mask of Tutankhamun and the Puntite relief figurine is the nemes headdress. The nemes is the striped head cloth worn by pharaohs in ancient Egypt. It covered the whole crown and back of the head and nape of the neck (sometimes also extending a little way down the back) and had two large flaps which hung down behind the ears and in front of both shoulders. It symbolized the Pharaoh's power[63].

[62] Silverman, David, (2003), Ancient Egypt, Oxford University Press, p. 242
[63] http://en.wikipedia.org/wiki/Nemes

Figure 11: "Puntite' king with crook, flail, divine osird beard, the nemes, the cobra snake and vulture. (Photo: Author)

Figure 12: King Tut's golden mask from his mummy with the flail and crook and displaying the divine osird beard, nemes, the cobra snake and vulture.

The *nemes* or the headdress is more visible in the below Puntite statuette, also found in Hargeisa. Again the cobra snake and vulture are mounted on the forehead while the *osird* beard is attached to the chin.

Ancient   Egyptians attached   special   sacred significance to many bird species and personified many of their major gods as birds. Some of those birds include the ibis, vulture, falcon/hawk (the sacred bird of Horus), heron, ostrich, and goose.

Figure 13: A 'Puntite' with a headgear and mounted with cobra, vulture and beard. (Photo: Mohamed A. Ali)

In a similar way, traditionally among Somalis, birds may have been sacred in the distant past; however, due to centuries of Islamic proselytism, what remains in the psyche of the people concerning birds are their association with and/or linking them to different attributes such as luck, misfortune, and in many instances as harbingers of good news, etc. Many of the Puntite statuettes, as the one inserted above (see fig. # 13) are mounted with a cobra snake and a vulture which are the same two creatures found in the Egyptian art form.

The following two statuettes are of two young men - an Egyptian and a Puntite. The shaven head of the Egyptian (King Tutankhamun) and the strange hair-do of the Puntite is a typical style that has been popular among the Somalis. The Puntite has a cross-shaped hair, part of the scalp left unshaven, appears as a band of hair linking one ear to the other, and another band from the forehead to the back of the head. Somalis believe that shaving a child's head clean can promote body growth and the recovery process of an ailing person as all available bodily energy is channelled towards that end. Head elongation was a common feature among Ancient Egyptians. But comparing this with the Puntites found so far – many of them shows vertical head elongation and even sometimes made into the form of crocodile, while the Ancient Egyptians had a somewhat horizontal elongation.

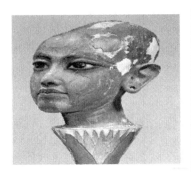

Figure 14: Young Tutankhamun (left), and a 'Puntite' with upright elongated head. (Photo sources: Tut's bust: touregypt.net; the Puntite bust: (Photo: Author)

The strange cranium formation among Ancient Egyptians may not have been natural but rather something induced and born from constant applying of external force by nursing mothers. Cranial deformation was a cultural preference among many races around the world and was probably performed to signify group affiliation[64], or to demonstrate social status.   Artificial cranial deformation was once commonly practiced in a number of cultures widely separated geographically and chronologically and still occurs today in a few places, like Vanuatu.[65] Until recently, artificial cranial deformation among many African communities was also known.

---

[64] Gerszten and Gerszten, 1995; Hoshower et al., 1995; Tubbs, Salter, and Oaks, 2006.
[65]wikipedia.org/wiki/Artificial_cranial_deformation

Figure 15: Two busts of Nefertiti, one with royal headdress, and the other without.

Figure 16: A Puntite statuette from Hargeisa valley with elongated head. (Photo: Mohamed A. Ali)

One of the oldest Ancient Egyptian deities is Sobek – the crocodile god which is often depicted as a crocodile, often in the form of a mummified crocodile or a man with the head of a crocodile. The strength and speed of the crocodile was thought to be symbolic of the power of the Pharaoh, and the word "sovereign" was written with the hieroglyph of a crocodile. It was thought that Sobek could protect the Pharaoh from dark magic. [66] Let me now present the supposed Puntite equivalent of the crocodile god. We have statuettes excavated from Hargeisa with vertically elongated heads made into the form of a crocodiles.

Figure 17: A figurine with a crocodile head excavated from a suburb of Hargeisa. (Photo: Author)

Yet another striking close relationship between the newly discovered 'Puntites' and ancient Egyptians figurines is the application of *kohl*[67] as an eye and eyebrow liner made from black galena (lead sulphide). It may have been mixed with water and gum, particularly myrrh, to form a paste.[68] Wore,

---

[66] http://www.ancientegyptonline.co.uk/sobek.html

[67] kohl: from Arabic *kohl*, a black powder made of antimony or lead sulphide.

[68] Somalis make their traditional ink for writing on wooden slates for religious instruction from a powdered

regardless of gender or status, ancient Egyptians believed that cosmetics had magical power to ward off evil and protect their eyes from eye diseases. *Kohl* application was also a funerary item. Figurines displaying kohl on their eyebrows are among those statuettes found in Somaliland.

Figure 18: A Puntite figurine wearing Kohl on eyes and brows. (Photo: Author)

According to ancient records eye paint was imported to Egypt. For example, an unidentified *eye-cosmetic* was brought from Punt by Hatshepsut's expedition together with, among other things, *ihmut-incense, sonter-incense,* apes and monkeys, etc.[69] Other sources

---

charcoal, diluted with water and added with powdered myrrh to form it into a paste and make it long lasting.
[69] Source: *Ancient records of Egypt; historical documents from the earliest times to the Persian conquest.* Andover-Harvard Theological Library, 1910, Cambridge, Massachusetts

of some ancient Egyptians cosmetic materials were from Coptos (Koptos)[70] and western Asia.[71]

Another interesting observation in the above statuette is the missing or half-missing arms, and comparatively there exists in the Ancient Egyptian art a life-sized mannequin or an effigy of King Tut which shows his upper torso and head, but without any arms. Such armless statuettes were also popular in the Grecian art, and the best example is that of Venus de Milo.

In the ancient Egyptian funerary processes, Canopic jars, made from stone or ceramic material was used for storing the inner organs which were removed during embalmment. The organs were preserved with the belief that they will be put into good use in the afterlife. They consisted of four jars; each receptacle came to be assigned to one of the four sons of Horus[72] and contained stomach, the intestines, the lungs, and the liver. In one location, not far from

---

[70] Coptos (Qift): A small town along the Nile in Upper Egypt, 43 km from Luxor.

[71] *Studies in Ancient Technology*, Volume III, (Brill Archive), p.18.

[72] The four sons of Horus: Imsety, Duamutef, Hapi, Qebehsenuef. The four sons of Horus were a group of four gods in Egyptian religion, who were essentially the personifications of the four canopic jars, which accompanied mummified bodies.

Hargeisa the author found four jars made of ceramic cupped with covers made from the same material.

Some commonalities between Somalis and Ancient Egyptians

It is becoming more common, during the recent years, to learn an increase in the number of western scholars finding it difficult to swallow the argument in favour of the mainstream scholarship on the origin of ancient Egyptians and their civilization as Indo-European. Many of these scholars assert the African roots of ancient Egypt. Examples of these are in the monumental works of Robert Bauval and Thomas Brophy's *Black Genesis* on one hand, and Martin Bernal in his *Black Athena*, on the other. In the same vein, the archaeological finds presented in the book will attempt to confirm the validity of such later ground-breaking scholarly works, which are in many instances seen controversial. The *Black Genesis* argues that the ancient Egyptian civilization did not come from the nowhere, but rather taken a gradual process which had its origins in the Sahara Desert. It hypotheses that the desert dwellers were Africans who practiced astronomical implements and calculations that have been later used in building the Pyramids. Worthy of mention here is the discovery of Nabta Playa archaeological site with its circular assembly of huge stone slaps which are believed, in terms of their alignment, to have astronomical significance. Some scholars, for example Professor J. McKim Malville of the University of Colorado and others believe that Nabta Playa culture may have stimulated the growth of the society that eventually constructed the first pyramids along the Nile about 4500 years ago.[73] The drying of the desert triggered the movement of the desert people to the Nile Valley to sow the seeds of one of the most advanced ancient civilizations of all time. The iconoclastic *Black Athena* equally suggests that classical civilization of Egypt in fact had deep roots in Afro-asiatic cultures, but misrepresented as Indo-European in origin.

In a peer-reviewed article, by S. O. Y. Keita, from the Department of Biological Anthropology in Oxford University, while analysing the claims and counter claims regarding the origin of ancient Egypt, he brings a strong argument in which he draws the attention of the reader to the North Eastern Africa. He argues that cranial and limp studies of ancient Egyptians indicated greater similarity to Somalis, Cushites and Nubians than with ancient Greeks. He further adds that this East African anatomy, once seen as being the result of a mixture of different "races," is

---

[73] http://wysinger.homestead.com/nabtaplaya.html

(as of late) better understood as being part of the range of indigenous African variations.[74]

Until recently, the mainstream denial of the ethnic identity of the Puntites as Africans by western scholars has continued to thrive unchallenged. The most popular justification for this is to establish a racial barrier among Africans with the colour and feature degradations by labelling them as 'Bantu', 'Nilote', 'Hamites' etc. to an extent that the later were branded as 'black-skinned' whites.[75]

In connection with the above, and in an attempt to establish a validity to describe the Puntite Somalis merely as 'black-skinned' whites and, but not 'true' Africans, Emmet Scott, the author of *Hatshepsut, Queen of Sheba*, quoted Amelia Ann Blanford (1891) whereby the later remarked upon the peculiar body shape of Queen Ati of Punt and the overall similarity of the present-day Somalis with Puntites as well:

> "(Gaston) Maspero suggests that the Princess Ati may be suffering from elephantiasis; but Mariette is of the opinion that the Egyptian artist has here represented not merely the wife of the Chief, but the

[74] Keita, S.O.Y., *Studies and comments on ancient Egyptian biological relationships*. History in Africa 20:129-154. 1993

[75] Edith Sanders, The Hamitic Hypotheses: Its Origin, and Functions in Time Perspective. Journal of African History, x, 4 (1969), pp. 521-532

most admired type of women of the Somali race. The complexion of {her} whole family is painted a brick red, thus showing that they are not of the negro race".[76]

Emmet Scott seems to be so ardent to run away with the Land of Punt and locate it in Asia, and particularly in Israel. In the opening sentence of a chapter in her book titled *'Ethnic Identity of the Puntites'*, she raises this question:

"This brings us to the second supposedly irrefutably African element, namely the Negros. How are they to be explained if we locate Punt in Asia?"[77]

Emmet Scott, was influenced by Immanuel Velikovsky's hypothesis of locating Punt in Israel, and challenging the 'fairly unanimous' consensus of putting Punt at the Southern end of the Red Sea in Eritrea and Somalia, or a combination of these two places, which she even further went to describe as 'primitive land' in Hatshepsut's time. Again she writes:

"Yet... there is no archaeological justification for such a supposition. Not a trace of anything that could be construed as implying Egyptian rule, even

---

[76] Emmet Scott, *Hatshepsut, Queen of Sheba*. Algora Publishing (2012), p. 90
[77] Ibid., 89

substantial contact with Egypt, has ever appeared {in those areas}."[78]

For the moment, her argument stands on a flimsy ground in the light of the archaeological material presented in this book.

The linguistic, cultural and physical similarities between Somalis and ancient Egyptians have been a subject of discussion among some scholars. Mohamed Hussein Abby discussed the cultural, belief, linguistic and products of the Land of Punt in his paper, *The Land of Poun* (Abby 2009). The list of Somali words in the annex of this book and their corresponding Egyptian equivalents is a fraction of the etymological similarities.

Maro, the traditional dress of Somali women, sadly not seen any more in the public arena, is a sheet of cloth wrapped intricately around the body with an elegant shoulder knot, a colourful sash dangling from the waist down *(Boqor)*, and a decorative belt with a plum dangling from the side *(dhacle)* which is very similar to the attire of early Egyptian women. Other than the similarity of attire, a simple scrutiny of the names of the king and the queen of Punt (Parehou and Ati) closely resemble the two popular Somali names namely "Barre" and "Utiya". Interestingly and

---

[78] Ibid., p. 93

coincidently, the literal meaning of "Utiya" means in Somali "a fat women who walks in a way she puts much effort in carrying her weight either due to obesity or to age". Compare this with the shape of queen Ati of Punt, as seen on the bas relief of Deir-el-Bahri, which raised a number of questions about her condition as to whether she is naturally obese or inflicted with some form of a disease. Historians are fairly unanimous that the cause of her condition can be related to a disease known as elephantiasis, which is characterized by the enlargement of a part of the body. But Mariette is of the opinion that the Egyptian artist has here represented not merely the wife of the chief, but the most admired type of the women of the Somali race.[79]

---

[79] Amelia Edwards, *Pharaohs Fellahs and Explorers.* Chapter 8: Queen Hatasu, and Her Expedition to the Land of Punt." New York: Harper & Brothers, 1891. (First edition.)

Figure 19: The image of Queen Ati of Punt, as depicted on Deir el Bahri walls

The king wears a kilt made of hide, equivalent to the Somali *dhuu* and a dagger (*toorray*). The appearance of the wiry men, with their hair plastered with lime (seen on some panels at Deir-el-Bahri) is till to this day a common feature among Somalis in the rural areas.

The pre-dynastic Egyptians where closely related to the people of the Horn of Africa. According to Ibrahim Ali (1993), when ancient Egyptian skulls are compared with the Somalis and Tigraeans, the coefficient of racial likeness indicated a close relationship. This is not surprising since the ancient

Egyptians regarded Somalia, the Land of Punt, as the home of their ancestors. [80] The common physical looks between the ancient Egyptians and the Puntites was also noted by Edouard Naville whose interpretation of the Deir-el-Bahri *bas reliefs* caused him to reach the conclusion that the Puntites were of two races which neither type represented with the characteristic colour and features of the negro, but regarding both types as belonging to Cushitic or Hamitic race, akin to the Egyptian and probably of the same common origin. [81] Naville mentions that there existed a trade between those coming from the interior, down to the coast land of Punt. He goes further to mention that the people of Ilim came with the Puntites to greet the visiting Egyptians. [82] The word "Ilim" is very similar to "ilin" (*cilin*) which means "a dwarf person" in Somali. Dwarfs and pygmies from the interior of Africa were sold (through Punt) into Egypt as slaves. This might allude to the two 'Hamitic' races of Ilim and Punt mentioned by Naville in the foregoing paragraph. In ancient Egypt, dwarfs were valued by the Pharaohs for their dancing skills and highly regarded as

---

[80] Ibrahim Ali, *the Origin and History of the Somali People*, Vol. I, p 22.

[81] Edouard Naville, *the Temple of Deir el Bahari: Its Plan, its Founders, and its First Explorers*. P. 24)

[82] Ibid., 23

dancers on special occasions and during religious festivals. There were at least two dwarf gods, Ptah and Bes. The god Ptah was associated with regeneration and rejuvenation while Bes was a protector of sexuality, childbirth, women, and children.[83]

Now, we can bring into this debate the controversy over the race and origin of ancient Egyptians, which has divided many scholars along racial lines. An important bone of contention is the race of the nineteen year old King Tutankhamun, to an extent that his face was reconstructed. Using CT-scan, the resultant head of the boy king was branded as North African as urged by Susan Anton, the leader of the American team working on the mummy. She noted that the shape of the cranial cavity indicated an African, while the nose opening suggested narrow nostrils, which is usually considered to be a European characteristic. Hence, the investigation concluded that the skull could be that of a North African. [84]

Now, with all the evidential material presented in this book on the subject matter, I can boldly say that that

---

[83] Chahira Kozma, Dwarfs in Ancient Egypt (Historical Review). American Journal of Medical Genetics (2005)
[84] 'A New Look at King Tut." An article by Guy Gugliotta, Washington Post, 11 May, 2005.

Tutankhamun was a Puntite by origin, who, at the same time, strikingly resembled the present-day Somalis. The physical looks of Somalis fit the above description generated by the CT-scan: They (Somalis) have the cranial skull of Africans on one hand, and aquiline nose and narrow nostrils, on the other!

Figure 20: Puntites loading the marvels of Punt on the Egyptians ships as depicted on Deir el Bahri walls.

The so-called "reddish-brown" colour of ancient Egyptians is not something alien among the Somalis who have various shades of colour, from jet black to fair skin. Traditional Somali names were very descriptive and not just picked randomly like it is the case of today where most of the names are of Arab origin. Traditional names and/or nicknames were given to an infant, child or a youth on the basis of a wide range of reasons such as, the time of birth, season, drought, rain, trekking, war, colour tone, character, etc. Hence, the Somali proverb *"Magac bilaash uma baxo"* (there must be a good reason for name giving). In the case of skin tones common names such as the following were popular among Somalis:

Name	Gender
Cawl (light brown)	Male
Casood (brown-reddish)	Male
Sagal (twilight)	Female/male
Siraad (illumination)	Male/female
Kaaha (shining)	Female
Sugulle (deep dark)	Male
Dhuxul (charcoal)	Male
Dhool (rain bearing cloud)	Female

From the above, the skin tone of Somalis range from light-brown to very dark, while having reddish brown is also uncommon.

How about the red hair colour found in many of ancient Egyptian mummies? Simply perform a Google search and study the head of any henna dyed hair of a Somali elder and his features. One can unmistakably easily attribute such features to some of the mummies in Egypt, particularly with Ramses II, the most influential and most powerful king that ever ruled Egypt. Henna (*Lowsonia inermis*), {*Cillaan* in Somali, pronounced as Elaan} is an indigenous plant that is found along the banks of seasonal water courses. The leaves contain *lowsone*, a pigment which is responsible for the red colour, which is used for colouring grey hair and decorating the skin and fingernails of women.

Piecing together the Punt Puzzle

The discovery of the Puntite artefacts may, at the same time, shed a new light on the movement of peoples and languages and, in particular, lead to the development of a new hypothesis on the original location of the Afro-asiatic family of languages. Different scholars placed the idea of what is called the Urheimat[85] of Afro-asiatic languages in various parts of Africa.[86] The present archaeological findings could also lead to the knowledge of a long history of human presence and ancient civilization in the *Waaqooyi*

---

[85] *Urheimat*: is a linguistic term that denotes the homeland of the speakers of a proto-language
[86] Bernal, Martin, *Black Athena*: The Afro-asiatic Roots of Classical Civilization - Vol. 3, New Brunswick, NJ, (1987) p. 72

which may contribute to changing the course of recorded history relating to the region.

The spiritual connection between the early Egyptians and the Puntites could further be confirmed by these discoveries. The land of Punt was not only the ancestral homeland of Pharaohs but at the same time the similarity between the Puntites and ancient Egyptians, in terms of physical looks, culture, worship and language is an indication that they may have been one and the same people. The Land of Punt must have been the cradle of the Egyptian civilization. As can be grasped from the comparison of those statuettes, the Puntite artefacts look similar, but cruder and less refined than those found in Egypt. Such refinement could be a result of further mastery of the art of craft making in Ancient Egypt. The ancient Egyptian civilization may have originated from its humble beginnings in the Golis Range (*Waaqooyi* = the Land of gods), including Hargeisa, evolving later in Egypt to one of the most sophisticated past civilizations of all times. The reason behind the name "gods' Land" is linked to the presence of the aromatic products which Egyptians always held in high regard, as "smelling pleasant was said to please the gods" (Shapland 2010). Having said this, here we can raise a question as to what

caused a section of the same people to depart from
The Land of gods to settle initially in Upper Egypt.

Whatever the reason might be, it is again very clear
that that the connection between the departees
(ancient Egyptians) and those who were left behind
(Puntites) remained strong. From the words of Queen
Hatshepsut who reigned over Egypt from 1473 to
1458 B.C. we can learn the feeling of nostalgia the
Pharaohs had for their ancestral home:

> "It is the sacred region of God's Land; it is my place
> of distraction; I have made it for myself in order to
> cleanse my spirit, along with my mother,
> Hathor...the lady of Punt."[87]

What a lofty expression of homesickness coming from
the lips of Queen Hatshepsut! Remember, the name
'Land of gods' has it's equivalent in Somali, i.e.
'Waaqooyi', and equally Hathor is represented (as
noted earlier) in the Laas Geelian rock art.

The above mentioned connection as well as the
likelihood that the aboriginal land of ancient
Egyptians was the Land of Punt, and their departure
to the Nile Valley has been proposed by William M.
Flinders Petrie, as early as the last years of the
eighteenth century. It is a known fact that he is

---

[87] http://www.egypttravel.net/blog/?p=4878

credited for the discovery of the pre-dynastic and Early Dynastic Egypt through his pioneering excavations of major sites such as Koptos, Naqada, and Abydos. He also believed that the founders of Egyptian civilization came from outside the country. In the Oriental Institute Museum Publication (33)[88], an important reference on him was made on this matter:

"In 1893/1894, he [Flinders Petrie] obtained from the *Service des Antiquites* permission to excavate at Koptos, where he believed the 'dynastic race' would have first settled in the Nile Valley after entering Egypt through the Wadi Hammamat from the Red Sea.... In 1894 he started work at the site of Naqada, where he was finally to find the evidence he so desired of turning out to contain an immense cemetery, in which Petrie and his team cleared over 2,000 graves... The dead had been placed in graves covered over originally with brushwood and low mounds of earth that had collapsed onto the burials... Most of the bodies were in foetal position – unlike the extended burials of the dynastic period – but with their faces to the west, indicating that they shared the Egyptian theory of 'the west' being the abode of the dead."

---

[88] Emily Teeter, *Before the Pyramids*, Oriental Institute Museum, USA, Publication # 33).

Again, an interesting observation in the occurrence
of cairn graves, almost in all parts of the Somali Golis
mountainous areas and the coastal belt as well, which
forms   the   northern   belt,   otherwise   known   as
Waqooyi[89]. In form, these structures, which are locally
known as *'Maguuro'* look like mini pyramids, with
their occupants buried in a manner which indicate the
belief in the rebirth after death, containing funerary
materials and belongings.

The skeletal remains shown in the following plate
(fig. 21) was unearthed by an archaeological team
from the British Institute in East Africa in 1976 in
Hafun (Xaafuun) - a promontory at the easternmost
point of the Somali Peninsula just to the south of Ras
Guardafui headland.   Hafun is the same place in
Somalia where Petrie said about it that "The Pun
{Punt} people founded the island fortress of Ha-fun,
which commands the whole of that coast, and hence
came the Punic or Phoenic peoples of classical
history."[90]

---

[89] Waaqooyi = Is meant here the northern mountainous
parts of the Somali Peninsula, or otherwise *"Dhulkii
Waaqyada"* (the Land of gods).
[90] Petrie, W.M. Flinders. *The Making of Egypt*, London. New
York, Sheldon Press; Macmillan, 1939. P.77

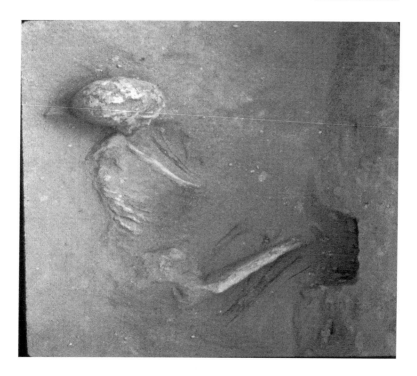

Figure 21: A skeleton remains from a grave near Hafun, Somalia. (Photo courtesy: British Institute in East Africa)

Hafun is also the Opone mentioned in the Periplus of the Erythraean Sea.[91]   The burial shows a contracted skeleton in a foetal position, with knees drawn up. In the same grave, one intact glazed pot was also found.

From the above quote by Petrie, the mention of "Punic" and "Phoenic" peoples and their relation with Hafun in Somalia is based on what is called the "Dynastic Race Theory" which its proponents claim

---

[91] Schoff, W. H., Text, Translation and Annotation of the Periplus of the Erythraean Sea (1912).

that Mesopotamians conquered and settled in Egypt, imposing themselves on the native Badarian culture to become their rulers, and then were responsible for the dynastic civilization. This theory has been very popular among Egyptologists in the 1950's but later challenged by the rise of Afro-centrists such as Cheikh Anta Diop, Martin Bernal, Robert Bauval and others. The Dynastic Race Theory is no longer an accepted thesis in the field of Pre-dynastic Archaeology, while modern technologies allowed the investigation of the DNA of the Egyptian peoples, and also found no evidence of significant Mesopotamian ancestry.[92]

The above skeletal remains and the one inserted hereunder (one found in Hafun, Somalia, and the other at Naqada in Upper Egypt) show great similarity. From the above, the possible absence of the Mesopotamian ancestry of ancient Egyptians, and equally the most likely absence of 'foreign' presence in the Somali Peninsula on one hand, and the very likelihood that it is the Land of Punt – the aboriginal home of ancient Egyptians – the African roots of the later is something which its argument and evidence cannot be easily refuted.

---

[92] Toby A. H. Wilkinson, *Early Dynastic Egypt*, pg 15

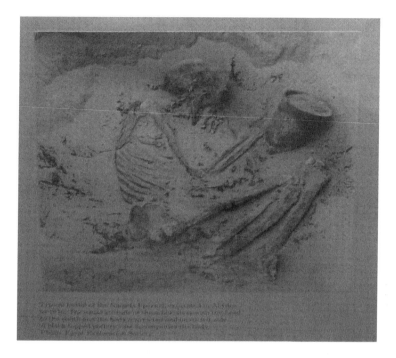

Figure 22: Typical burial of the Naqada period in Egypt. (Photo courtesy: Egypt Exploration Society)

Interestingly, the near proximity of Naasa Hablood twin mountains to Hargeisa which are very similar in shape with the Egyptian pyramids on one hand, and the finding of Puntite artefacts in the valley cannot be just brushed off as a coincidence. The departees from Punt, who settled, initially, in Upper Egypt had to maintain their link with the Land of Punt not only through remembrance and occasional visits, but also by keeping that memory alive by erecting structures that could remind them of the Land of gods. In this case, the pyramids were built not only as huge burial structures but at the same time to remind them of their ancestral home, and specifically Naasa Hablood Twin Mountains and the nearby valley where many of those Pharaonic-like busts presented in this book came from.

Figure 23: Pyramid-shaped Nasa Hablood mountains of Hargeisa city. (Photo by the author)

The same can be said about the Europeans who were either put into exile or, in most cases, moved voluntarily to distant lands namely Australia or the Americas. They kept memories of their ancestral homes alive by creating miniature replica of something dear to them which they left behind, or calling their new settlements the same names they had back home. Few examples of these are New Caledonia, New Zealand, New York, New Hampshire, New England, etc.

Budge, E. A. Wallis, in his attempt to answer the following question: Who were they (ancient Egyptians)? To what race did they belong? If they were immigrants, where did they come from? He took the human remains that have been found in Neolithic graves of Egypt as a reference point. He opined that they were Africans. Also the Egyptian tradition of the Dynastic period held that the aboriginal home of the ancient Egyptians was Punt. However, he gave the credit of ancient Egyptian civilization to new comers whose bodies 'contained more brains than those of their predecessors in Egypt... and were (that) men who built the Pyramids and all the other mighty works in stone'. He argued that 'it is quite certain that many of their physical characteristics were "European"... and they conquered (the natives) with great success, making themselves masters of all the Egyptian portion of the Valley of the Nile.' However, he mentioned one big weakness which compromises his argument:

> "But though they were great and powerful conquerors, and mighty builders, they never succeeded in altering the fundamental beliefs and manners and customs of the bulk of the natives Egyptians (Africans), for these continued to worship their African Gods, and to bury their dead, and to

live in the same way as their ancestors had lived for thousands of years before them".[93]

After all, if we go for Jared Diamond's hypothesis, in his *Guns, Germs and Steel,* on why Europeans conquered the world, he documents the fate of many races in the South that have been conquered and dominated both physically and mentally. Expansion of culture and beliefs went hand in hand with the physical domination through raids. Yet, the contradictory part of Budge's above statement, compared to the Diamond's hypothesis, is that the 'Europeans' could not succeed in diffusing their culture and beliefs even after exerting their physical dominance over them, but, on the contrary, adopted the 'African' culture and religion in wholesale. The question is: How could these conflicting hypotheses be reconciled? If the 'Europeans' were so 'smart' why they did not foist their beliefs on the conquered or rather influence the culture and psyche of the oppressed and the defeated? If the dominant class where racially Caucasoid, why, rather than frequenting an African destination as a Land of Punt, did not they have a European or even Asian Punt? In my opinion, Jared Diamond's argument is relatively more reasonable. Diamond did not attribute the

---

[93] Budge, E. A. Wallis, A Short History of the Egyptian People, pg 13

success of the 'Europeans' on racial issues, but on geography and the right environment at the right time. In nutshell, from the analysis of the above argument, it is certainly clear that the origin of the ancient Egyptian civilization is rooted in the African continent.

Within Africa too, one of the arguments against the Somali peninsula being the Land of Punt appeared in a report published on the internet claiming to have finally proved Eritrea being the ancient Punt. The said argument originated from a research team consisting of American scientists who investigated the mummies of baboons (*Papio hamadryas*) said to have been imported from Punt. As per the report, testing of hair from the baboons, using oxygen isotope analysis, revealed where the animals had originated. The study ruled out Somalia and Yemen while, it said, that the isotope values in baboons from Eritrea and neighbouring Ethiopia were closely matched. It is worth noting that baboons are very common in the Somali peninsula and have even multiplied in the past few decades as result of the numerical decline of its natural enemy – the leopard.

In the absence of archaeological evidence, the above research findings might be good enough to be entertained, but given the more or less credible findings coming out from Somaliland, a country which has not been subject to any meaningful archaeological excavation, such hypothesis does not stand on a firm ground. Moreover, the weakness of the above claim lies in the fact that it ignores that these creatures (like others, including plant species) migrate as a result of changes in climate patterns, and therefore, the localization of Punt in that area (Eritrea) is still vague. Climate change continued in the past and continues in the present time to drive the region to aridity. The Neolithic cave painting of Laas Geel in Somaliland (see fig. 5) depict humpless bovines which are not currently found anywhere in Somaliland/Somalia. Also, rock shelters at Karin Heegane, a natural mountain pass approximately 70 kilometres southwest of Bosaso contains extensive rock paintings (Brandt, Brook, and Gresham 1983, p.16). The most important feature of rock painting panels at Karin Heegane is a type of cattle, today extinct in the Somali-inhabited areas, but found in Egypt, called *jamuusa*.[94] In the last forty years, because of the recurring droughts and chaotic situation in Somalia, local communities believe that migration of wildlife species to neighbouring countries has taken place over time. Similarly, over

---

[94] Mohamed Diriye Abdullahi, "Cushites: North-eastern Africa: Stone Age Origins to Iron Age," in Kevin Shilligton (ed.), Encyclopaedia of African History, vol. 1, pp. 566-568. (2004)

the past several millennia, so much has changed in the composition of vegetation in the Somali peninsula. The discovery of rocks made into the form of crocodiles in Hargeisa valley could be an indication of a tropical riparian ecosystem to have existed in those areas. Therefore, it cannot be discounted that ebony, one of the chief exports from Punt, was sourced from the area. *Diospyros sp.*, locally known as 'Kolaati', is still found to a limited extent in riparian formations in Somalia.

I have already discussed in the foregoing sections how some of the Puntite figurines presented in this book carry items which echo as a true representation of the ancient Egyptian royal regalia such as the crook *(heka)*, flabellum *(nekhakha)*, osird beard, the royal cobra *(uraeus)* and vulture. Also, the similarity of the funerary processes of the Puntites and ancient Egyptians can be gleaned from the use *kohl,* as well as the canopic jars used by the ancient Egyptians during the preparation of their dead for the afterlife. Both races (Puntites and ancient Egyptians) maintained the belief that having the bodies of their dead to their likeness through representation in images helped secure their place in the afterlife. Ancient Egyptians believed the deceased body would have to resemble the past living body as much as possible so the *ka* could recognize its body and then the *ba* would "return to it each night after spending time in the sunshine."[95]

Here I would like to refer to an interesting question raised by Shapland (2010) concerning the cordial relationship between the Egyptians and Puntites. He writes: *'While there were many close allies, important trading partners, and sworn enemies to the Egyptian Empire, there does not seem to be a relationship as ambiguous as Punt's. Why did the Egyptians hold such obvious respect for them (Puntites)?"* He also mentions that while the Egyptians depicted foreigners in their art as lawless, unstable and inferior, and according to their aspective art practices, smaller in stature than themselves, Puntites are respectfully drawn equal in size.

According to my understanding, the 'ambiguous relationship' most likely could mean that they were one and the same people. Budge, E. A. Wallis said an

---

[95] According to ancient Egyptian belief, *Ka* and *Ba* were two spiritual entities that everyone possessed. Their belief were that the living were responsible to help the dead journey to the Afterlife. "The *Ka* was essentially a person's double", it was the life force and at death it was separated from the body. The Ba, was seen as a human-headed bird hovering over the deceased.. and was part of the soul that could travel between the worlds of the living and the dead. (Source: Mortuary Practices of Ancient Egypt. http://myweb.usf.edu/~liottan/theegyptiansoul.html)

interesting remark about this relationship whereby he mentioned that the Egyptian expeditions "brought back myrrh and other products of the country, which were so dear to the heart of *kinsmen* of the Puntites who were settled in Egypt".[96] While the Egyptian expeditions were seen well-armed when interacting with the Puntites, there is no sign of hostility to be sensed from those silent expressions that can be seen on the *bas reliefs* of Deir-el-Bahri. The people of Punt were seen as peaceful trade partner rather than a chaotic enemy. However, the Egyptians, who might have known the unpredictable character of the Puntites, did not want to take any risk of being caught off guard by being unarmed. The turbulent and hostile nature of the Puntites, or those who came after them, like the present day Somalis, has been documented by many ancient travellers. The unknown author of *The Periplus of the Erythraean Sea* describes the people of 'the Other Barbaria" (i.e. Somalis), as "very unruly" (Chap. 7, *the Periplus*) while describing those who lived in Mundus, the present day (Maydh/Mait) on the Somali coast, as "very quarrelsome". (Chap. 9, *the Periplus*). Another interesting description in *the Periplus* reads as follows *"the country is not subject to a king, but each market-town has its own chief"* (Chap. 14). That is a true reflection of

---

[96] Budge, E. A. Wallis, A short History of Egyptian People. (1914) London. Pg. 10

the current schism prevailing in the length and breadth of the Somalia proper. Such quarrelsomeness and aggressive nature of Somalis made their land inhospitable for any foreign people to colonize their country or monopolize their commerce as reported by Tuan Ch'eng Shih, the 9th century Chinese traveller who visited the land of *Po-pa-li* (commonly translated as Berbera/Somalis).[97]

Let us now compare this with the descriptions made by one European among many who became confused by the character of the Somali and who could not equally contradict a similar impression formed by Richard Burton (1854). Major Rayne (1921) describes Somalis 'a people whose psychology it is impossible for a European mind, with no experience of them, to understand and explain. To the average European, and nearly to all other African tribes, the name of Somali is anathema.'[98]

On the basis of the foregoing narration, no wonder that the early Egyptians had to arm themselves to the teeth in their expeditions to the Land of Punt.

The presence of Puntites in Hargeisa valley (roughly 145 km south of the Gulf of Aden from the nearest

---

[97] Ibrahim Ali, *the Origin and History of the Somali People*, pp. 42, Vol. I, (1993)
[98] Rayne, Major M. C. H., (1921), Sun, Sand and Somalis.

point 'Bullaxaar' straight north to the sea) could mean that the Puntites had even ventured deeper into the African hinterland. This could be an answer and a clue to the exportation of slaves and particularly dwarfs and pygmies from the Land of Punt to ancient Egypt. Therefore, trade network of the Puntites reached as far as the Congo basin, and the ancient gold mining colony of Mashonaland in the present-day Zimbabwe.[99] This underlines the likelihood that Punt may have played an intermediary role in the trade in the region. Another evidence to support this role is the prominence of cinnamon trade in the Somali peninsula, as recorded in *the Periplus of the Erythraean Sea*, whereby the sagacity of its inhabitants enabled them to source from the Far East and tranship it from the string of market towns on the coast of the Somali coast, also once known as 'the Land of the Cinnamon.'

The high demand for gold in ancient Egypt, and the necessity to diversify its source, forced the early Egyptians to push southwards into new frontiers in Nubia and beyond the second cataract on the Nile to exploit its vast gold deposits.[100] Also, not far from

---

[99] www.goldgold.com/gold-in-the-ancient-world.html
[100] Hiller, John, Gold in the Ancient World, the News 49'ers.

Hargeisa is the Arabsiyo area reported to have gold-quartz veins with gold content of up to 13.5 ppm.[101]

Waaq and *Weger* Worship

In this section, we will discuss the existence of two traditional religions in the Somali peninsula prior to the arrival of Islam in the region, one of which i.e. *Waaq* cult widely popular among historians and many peoples in the northern eastern Africa. Unfortunately, very little is known about the other cult, namely *Weger* worship. Until the recent discovery of the 'Puntites', the *Weger* stick (see fig. 24), which I will later explain some of its ritual practices, was the sole piece of artefact that can be attributed to some kind of worship from the past.[102]

---

[101] Bob Forester and Alexandra Harrison, Mining Annual Review (2000)

[102] Another reference to the existence of idol worship in the Somali lands is made by Ibraahin Yuusuf 'Hawd', a prolific Somali writer, in an article written in Somali titled "*Warqaddii Gabowday, Gabowday, Gabowday*" (the Ancient, ancient, most ancient letter). He said many years back, during his school days, while on trip to the old port town of Berbera, his uncle (Aw Abdullahi H. Jama) summoned him to read a very old letter written in Arabic on a medieval paper. According to Ibraahin, he understood that the letter was sent by a friend of Sheikh Isaaq (the eponym of the Isaaq tribe who probably returned from Makkah in Saudi Arabia after a sojourn in holy city for religious education). The friend left behind and the author of the

However, after unearthing those Puntite objects, a new era of archaeological interest, which will extend the *Weger* worship to the distant past is about to dawn. Likewise, this may also trigger some scholarly questions, such as, whether the two religions were practiced simultaneously by their adherents. And who were the people who carved those beautiful statuettes?

The reader may wonder the link between the Puntite/Egyptian discussions elaborated in this book and the subject I am about to introduce. In fact, this is only an attempt to link the *Weger* worship (a

letter was addressing Sheikh Isaaq. The message and tone of the letter was very cordial and carried a gesture of encouragement for the Sheikh to continue Islamic proselytism among Somalis with renewed fervour, while at the same time urging him to resist and fight back the idolaters and the Christians with ferocity. Sheikh Isaaq's arrival is dated at 12-13th Century CE.

In my opinion, the idolaters mentioned in the letter could be the *Weger* worshippers who could also be related to the Puntites. The total disappearance of the Puntite artefacts from the surface of the earth for such a long period of time, and their recent excavation from very shallow holes may indicate the prevalence of religious persecution whereby the hiding of the artefacts may have been carried out hurriedly. Ultimately, it is very logic that this may have prompted the carving of the *Weger* stick by the idolaters as a portable item of worship which remained till the present times to have some religious and superstitious significance.

traditional religion of polytheistic nature) to the religion of the Puntites. However, it is a question which requires further research how *Waaq* worship, which is generally believed to have strong elements of monotheism, co-existed with *Weger* worship.

Prior to the discovery of those Puntite statuettes and artefacts in many parts of Somaliland, the predominant belief among historians was that Waaq cult, with its monotheistic features, has been practiced by the Cushitic peoples, including Somalis. Yet, I was perplexed by the presence of a single wooden item (fig. 24) which is a relic locally believed by many to have been worshiped by Somalis, which also still defied disappearance – despite Islam's abhorrence to idol worship. Another reference that could allude to some kind of polytheistic deity is the traditional swearing on God's name *"Wallaahi, Billaahi, Tallaahi, Tinniixi iyo Tincaaro"* – as if the last two words stand for deities which existed in the Somali peninsula before the coming of Islam. *Weger* is a piece of wood, approximately 40 cm in length, made into a crude form of a human head with flattened 'checks' or sides, and with an elongated end which serves as a handle. Woodcrafters make the *Weger* stick from the heartwood of a tree with the same name. *Olea africana* can be found in the highest ecological zones of Golis Mountain Range. Because of its supposed magical powers, *Weger* stick is popular among pregnant women or those nursing infants as an evil neutralizer. Usually they keep it under pillows and carry with them when they go out of their homes. Fighting men also believed that throwing it at an approaching enemy may auger their defeat. It is regarded as a morale booster for a defendant or an accused person participating in an open Somali court session. The translation of the popular Somali exclamation *'Weger iyo ka waaweyn'* fit the English *"My God!"* or its Arabic equivalent *'Ya Ilaahi"*.

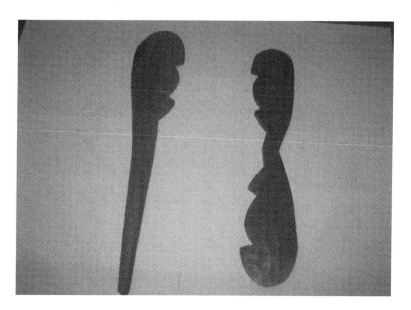

Figure 24: Weger stick crafted from Olea africana from Gacan Libaax Mountain in central Somaliland by a local craftsman. (Photo: Author)

On the other hand, it is a known fact among the historians that *Waaq* or *Waaqoo* stands for the Cushitic sky god. The *Waaq* cult also shared common characteristics with monotheistic religions. According to Jaylan W. Hussein,[103] *Waaqeffannaa* (belief in Sky god) was the traditional religion of the Oromo people, in general, and the Arsi, in particular. The Oromo name for Supreme Being is *Waaq* which has no representation with an image. The Oromo's belief in Sky god antedates both Christianity and Islam. The Oromo (and also the Somali) regard *Waaq* as the Owner and Sustainer of the universe (Bartels, 1983; Lewis, 1955, 1956). The Oromo had a sophisticated mythology of Creation, called *Uumaa* (*Uumee*)[104] who is perfect in His accomplishment of the creation process and a source of life and identity, self-sustaining and one who never lazed into neutrality after creating the world but at the same time intervenes in the day-to-day motion of His creatures (Jaylan, 2005).

To clear the confusion emanating from the above two contradictory 'beliefs', one characterized by clear

---

[103] Jaylan W. Hussein, *The functions of African oral arts: the Arsi-Oromo* (2005, Faculty of Education, Alemaya University, Ethiopia)

[104] Compare to the Somali word *"Uume"* which has the same meaning, but even referring not only to 'creation' but 'the starter and beginner of creation'.

element of monotheism (*Waaq* worship), and the other by polytheistic features in the form of the above *Weger* stick on one hand, and the growing material evidence exposed in this research as well, I strongly believe that *Weger* worship stands for a spiritual continuum linking it to the religion of the Puntites. There is an ample evidence of the existence of *Waaq* worship as a pre-Islamic indigenous religion practiced by Somalis as well as other Cushites such as the Afar, Beja and Agaw, Saho and Oromo.

The Somali language contains words describing place and/or tribal names, exclamatory remarks and some with religious significance that can be directly linked to the word 'Waaq'. The list can be exhaustive but here are few examples:

Garwaaqsi: To accept judgment, literally 'judgment of God'. It also means His judgment is the most just.

Ceel Waaq: Literally the 'well of God'. A town in the north-eastern province of Kenya – a region inhabited mainly by Somalis.

Caabud Waaq: Town in southwest Somalia, literally 'a place where God is worshipped'. It could have been a centre of learning and religious practice.

Waaq la': A deserted place, devoid of God's mercy.

Weligay iyo Waaqay [105] : Currently its meaning corresponds *to "never before did I ...."* It describes action or a thing that has no precedence. Like saying *"Weligay iyo waaqay isha maan saarin saan-caddaale, or {never before had I set an eye on a white man!}.* The phrase also might have been used for swearing before being replaced with *"Wallaahi, Billaahi iyo Tallaahi"*.

Cig Waaqe: A consolationary prayer addressed to someone afflicted with misfortune such as loss of a dear one. It means 'May God provide you with worthy replacement for what you had lost!'

Dhagax Waaq kugu dhac! A curse which literally means "May you be hit by a stone hurled from Heavens!"

Waqal: A cloud heavily laden with water which stands for mercy from above (from *Waaq* – Sky god).

---

[105] Comparatively, there is a verse in the Holy Qur'an which contains those two words (*Weliyin walaa Waaq*) whereby some people argue that the Somali version has been borrowed from the Holy Qur'an (Ra'ad: 37). However, the truth might be the other way round as the Arabic (like any other language) has absorbed foreign words which became Arabized before the coming of the Islamic revelation. On the other hand, since linguists trace the Somali and Arabic to the Erythraean family of languages, otherwise called Afro-asiatic, there is the possibility that both languages shared many common words such as *"weli"* and *"Waaq"*.

According to a local tradition, children are advised not to point their fingers directly at such clouds, lest they will scatter and the anticipated rain will fail. On such occasions pointing was done with a closed fist.

Barwaaqo: Literally 'a spot of God's rain'.

There are also dozens of names found in the genealogies of many tribes. Examples are _Jid Waaq_, _Tagaal Waaq_ and _Ga'al Waaq_.

Waaq can also be found in the mat weaving song:

> _Cawskanow sabool diidow,_
>
> **Waaq** _aan suuqa lagu dhigin oo_
>
> _Soddon lagugu baayicin oo_
> _Yaa sameeyay lagu odhon ee_
>
> _This mat is not for a poor man,_
>
> _God forbid that that you should be displayed for sale_
> _in the market,_
>
> _Bought with only thirty (coins),_
>
> _'Who made it'? They will ask![106]_

The Somali word 'Waaqooyi or Waqooyi' has two meaning: a) North direction; and b) the northern mountainous areas facing the Gulf of Aden. Since

---

[106] Cf with the translation by I. M. Lewis, Saints _and Somalis_. p. 138, the Red Sea Press, Inc. (1998)

Waaq (in Somali) and *Waaqoo* (in Oromo) are
equivalent to God, *Waaqooyi* is undoubtedly the Land
of gods!   Because of the past sacredness of those
northern mountainous areas, their relation to *Waaq*
can be fully justified. Many other place names in the
northern Somali coast and hinterland can be
identified with *Waaq* such as *Waaqeel* (a plain near
Gacan Libaax Mountain), *Waaqderiya* (on the coast
between Mait and Las Qoray), *Waaqderi* (near Las
Anod) and *Waaq Dhambala* (an estuary where
Waaheen seasonal watercourse enters the sea and
another location near Karin to the east of Berbera).

It could be that simple! *Waaqooyi* – a word which is as
ancient as the Somalis – means 'the land of gods'.
Therefore, the Land of Punt could be no other place
than *Waaqooyi* (the northern Somali coast).

Conclusion

In the search of the real location of the Land of Punt, the surfacing of those Puntite artefacts in Somaliland will put the limelight on a more probable location than any other area before in the past. These discoveries will also confirm the argument postulated by Auguste Mariette's during the last quarter of the nineteenth century in which he proposed that the Somali peninsula was the Land of Punt. Therefore, those concrete indicators might lead to unravel the long standing mystery. Moreover, it is high time to organize and conduct in-depth archaeological investigations in the *Waaqooyi* areas of the Somali Peninsula.

Even though no radiometric dating has been done on the 'Puntites' artefacts yet, and doubtlessly, they are findings of great antiquity which can be dated back to the pre-dynastic period of Egyptian history (5,500 to 3,100 BC). The great similarity between the products of the two peoples, particularly on how the statuettes were hewn, engraved, and the pigments used do not only show that there were racial, cultural and artistic commonalities, but at the same time they were two contemporary civilizations, with more likelihood that the Puntite civilization preceded the former.

The discovery of these artefacts will definitely contribute to enrich the humanity's common heritage and therefore, calls for an action to explore, investigate and safeguard this shared legacy. Many of the artefacts presented in this book were found in Hargeisa valley which has now been converted into a sprawling city of almost one million inhabitants and, at the same time, experiencing unprecedented land use alterations. Indiscriminate quarrying of rock activities for use in buildings is also threatening a unique, but also potentially rich untapped cultural heritage.

Finally, I hope this book will revive new interest in the search of the Land of Punt, whereby future research might proceed from an attitude of near-resignation, to an extent Punt has been expressed as something 'metaphysical', to something realistic and having physical existence.

Some common Somali words/meanings and their corresponding Egyptian words/meanings

Somali	Meaning	Egyptian	Meaning
Agas	Food consumed at the grave of a dead person and served to those carrying out the burial	Agas	Food
Af	Mouth	Af	Mouth/Greedy
Eey/Yey	Dog/jackal	Auau	Dog/jackal
Aagaan	Small milk container	Agn	Support of a vessel
Aqaar	Measure	Aqr	Measure
Fuqa	Nozzle	Fqa	Nozzle
Fuuqso	To sip something with a hissing sound	Feqq	To eat, to feed
Beri	To rise (sun), east	Per	To rise (of the sun)
Bakhbakh	To enjoy	Bakhbakh	To enjoy

Bakh	Action of dropping something from the female genital part or released the anus such as passing air	Bakh	To give birth
Bah	Self (in the form of air)	Bah	To inhale
Bes	Seriously ill	Bes	A disease of some kind which is accompanied by boils or sores or swelling
Besid	Flame dying out	Besid	Flame, fire, blaze
Besti	Seriously ill (masculine)	Basti	Unguent, ointment
Mujo	Infant	Muje	Infant
Dayax (h)	Moon	Yeah	Moon
Hees	Song	His	Song
Qaboob	Cold	Qbb	Cold

Nuunuu	Child	Nni	Child
Naf	Life	Nf	Life
Baas	Hawk	Pash	Kind of bird
Bar qabow	A place of coolness	Per Qebh	A place of coolness (refreshment)
Bisil	Cooked food	Pesit	Cooked food
Bashaq	The sound of spittle	Pessag	Spittle or to spit
Baqo	Be timid, coward	Peki	To be timid
Bad	Sea	Pet	Flood, inundation
Fakh	Unloose (like unloose a trap)	Fekh	Unloose, detach
Maro	Cloth	Mar	Cloth
Mahaa tidhi (maxaa tidhi)	What did you say?	M'h-t	Forgetfulness
Meher	Dowry	M'kher	Dowry
Wa Kaa	Behold! See! He is there!	M' ka	Behold ! See!

Index

Bibliography

Books and Articles

Ahmed Ibrahim Awale, *Dirkii Sacmaallada* (2012): *Meel-ka-soo-jeedka Soomaalidii Hore: Sooyaal, Rumayn, Ilbaxnimo.* Liban Publishers, Denmark.

Al-Houdalieh, Salah Hussein , *Archaeological Heritage and Spiritual Protection: Looting and the Jinn in Palestine,* Journal of Mediterranean Archaeology 25.1 (2012) 99–120

Bernal, Martin, *The Afro-asiatic Roots of Classical Civilization* - Vol. 3, New Brunswick, NJ, (1987).

Bob Forester and **Alexandra Harrison**, *Mining Annual Review (2000)*

Bauval, Robert and **Thomas Brophy**, *Black Genesis: The Prehistoric Origins of Ancient Egypt (2011)*

Budge, E. A. Wallis, *An Egyptian Hieroglyphic Dictionary (1920)*

Budge, E.A. Wallis, *Short History of the Egyptian People* 1914, Kessinger Publishing.

Chittick, N. *An Archaeological Reconnaissance of the Horn: The British-Somali Expedition'.* (1974)

Clark, J. D., *The Prehistoric Cultures of the Horn of Africa – An analysis of the Stone Age Cultural and Climatic Succession in the Somalilands and Eastern Parts of Abyssinia,* (1954), Cambridge University Press.

Crowther, Pete (2010), *Locating the Land of Punt – the Case for Eritrea* – Thesis, Certificate in Egyptology, University of Manchester.

Diop, Cheik Anta, *"Evolution of the Negro World"*, Presence Africaine, no. 51, (1964)

Diop, Cheik Anta, *The African Origin of Civilization: Myth or Reality.* Lawrence Hill Books, 1974

Emmet Scott, *Hatshepsut, Queen of Sheba.* Algora Publishing (2012).

Fattovich, **Rodolfo**, *Egypt's trade with Punt: New discoveries on the Red Sea coast, British Museum Studies in Ancient Egypt and Sudan 18 (2012): 1–59*

Glenister, Catherine Lucy, *Profiling Punt: Using Trade Relations to Locate 'God's Land'*, Ph.D. thesis. (2008)

Gufu Oba, Climate Change Adaptation in Africa: An Historical Ecology – A Historical Ecology, Routledge (2014)

Gutherz et. al. *The discovery of new rock paintings in the Horn of Africa : the rockshelters of Laas Geel,* Republic of Somaliland / Xavier Gutherz, Jean-Paul Cros & Joséphine Lesur. - 2003. - vol. 1, no. 2, p. 227-236 : foto's, krt - In: Journal of African Archaeology: (2003), vol. 1, no. 2, p. 227-236 : foto's, krt.

Gutheerz, Xavier, *the Decorated Shelters of Laas Geel and the Rock Art of Somaliland.* Presse Universitaries de la Mediterranee, September, 2011.

Hiller, John, *Gold in the Ancient World*, the News 49'ers.

Ib Friis, et. al,. *Biodiversity Research in the Horn of Africa, Proceedings of the Third International symposium* *on the Flora of Ethiopia and Eritrea,* Carlsberg Academy (2001), pg. 144

Ibrahim Ali, *The Origin and History of the Somali People,* pp. Vol. I, (1993).

Ibraahin Yuusuf Axmed "Hawd", *Sheeko Gaaban: Warqaddii Gabowday gabowday gabowday!.* (www.weedhsan.com).

Jacke Philips, 'Ancient Egypt: *Presynaptic Egypt and Nubia: Historical Outline',* in K. Shillington (ed), Encyclopaedia of African History`, Volume 1, pp. 399-401

Jacke Philips, *Punt and Aksum: Egypt and the Horn of Africa.* The Journal of African History, Vol. 38, No. 3 (1997), pp. 423-457

Keita, S. O. Y., *the Geographical Origins and Population Relationships of Early Ancient Egyptians,* Department of Biological Anthropology, Oxford University

Keita, S.O.Y., *Studies and comments on ancient Egyptian biological relationships.* History in Africa 20:129-154. 1993

K.O. Farah et.al, *The Somali and the Camel: Ecology, Management and Economics.* Anthropologist, 6(1): 45-55 (2004)

Marriete, Auguste, *Deir-el-Bahari.* Hichrichs, 1877

Michael Rice, *Egypt's Making: The Origins of Ancient Egypt 5000-2000 BC,* Second edition. Routledge (2003)

Mohamed Diriye Abdullahi, *"Cushites: Northeastern Africa: Stone Age Origins to Iron Age,"* in Kevin Shillington (ed.), Encyclopedia of African History, vol. 1, pp. 566-568. (2004)

Mohamed Hussein Abby (2009), *The Land of Poun (Punt),*

M. Y. Ali & I. Ibrahim, *Rock Art in Somaliland: Discovery of two new rock painting sites*, the Petroleum Institute, Abu Dhabi, UAE, Issue # 25, January, 2013.

Naville, Edouard (1894*): Deir el Bahari: Its plan, its founders, and its first explorers.* Egypt exploration fund. Vol. 12.

Pankhurst, Richard, *the Ethiopian Borderlands: Essays in Regional History from Ancient Times to the End of the 18th Century*. The Red Sea Press Inc. (1997) Asmara, Eritrea

Peter Tyson, *Where is Punt?*, Nova (2009).

Raphael Chijioke Njoku, *The History of Somalia*, (2013) Greenwood Books

Robson, Eric, (2007*) In Search of Punt: Queen Hatshepsut's Land of Marvels,* Shama Books.

Sada Mire, *The Discovery of Dhambalin Rock Art Site*, Somaliland 2008).

Rayne, Major M. C. H., (1921), Sun, Sand and Somals.

Sanders, Edith: *The Hamitic hypothesis: its origin and functions in time perspective*, The Journal of African History, Vol. 10, No. 4 (1969),

Sayed, A. M. A. H., *The Land of Punt: Problems of the Archaeology of the Red Sea and the South-eastern Delta,* University of Alexandria.

Schoff, W.H., Text, *Translation and Annotation of The Periplus of the Erythraean Sea, (1912)*

Silverman, David, (2003), *Ancient Egypt,* Oxford University Press

Sutton, J. E. G., *the Aquatic Civilization of Middle Africa,* Journal of African History, XV, 4, (1974).

Ward, Cheryl, *Building pharaoh's ships: Cedar, incense and sailing the Great Green.* British Museum Studies in Ancient Egypt and Sudan 18 (2012): 217–32

Wicker, F.D.P. (1998) *'The Road to Punt',* Geographical Journal, vol. 164, 1976. Pp. 45-56.

Other books by the author

1.   *Qaylo-dhaan Deegaan: Qoraallo Xulasho ah* (2010), (Environment in Crisis with Focus on Somali Environment). Ponteinvisible, Pisa, Italy.

ISBN #: 88-88934-13-8

2.   *Dirkii Sacmaallada* (2012): *Meel-ka-soo-jeedka Soomaalidii Hore: Sooyaal, Rumayn, Ilbaxnimo.* Liibaan Publishers, Denmark.

ISBN #: 978-87-995208-1-7

3.   *SITAAD: Is-dareen-gelinta Diineed ee Dumarka Soomaaliyeed (2013),* Liibaan Publishers, Denmark

ISBN #: 978-87-995208-2-4

4.   *Maqaddinkii Xeebaha Berri-Soomaali (2014),* Liibaan Publishers, Denmark

ISBN #: 978-87995208-3-1

Printed in Great Britain
by Amazon

16312473R00072